"Once upon a time, competitive advantage belonged to the people who knew the most. Now it accrues to those who know how to learn the most. In his new book, Brad Staats skillfully takes you through the latest evidence on how to accelerate your learning at work."

—**ADAM GRANT**, *New York Times*–bestselling author, *Give and Take*, *Originals*, and *Option B* (with Sheryl Sandberg)

"A brilliant tutorial in how we learn—or more often—how we don't. The essential guidebook to prepare for a new age."

—**GENERAL (RET) STANLEY McCHRYSTAL**, Commander, U.S. and International Security Assistance Forces in Afghanistan; bestselling author, *Team of Teams*

"In this astute work, Brad Staats describes the forces that are propelling us into an economy that values the ability to learn above all else. Using a mix of behavioral science and operations research, he demystifies the learning process and explains how each of us can become a dynamic learner. This book is essential reading for anyone hoping to learn faster and better."

—**DANIEL H. PINK**, author, *When* and *Drive*

"Brad Staats provides a practical road map to one of the biggest challenges facing leaders today. Now more than ever, the best leaders know they need to be lifelong learners in order to stay ahead of the curve. *Never Stop Learning* is packed with powerful insights and tips to help you master the art of learning."

—**MATT BREITFELDER**, Chief Talent Officer and Managing Director, BlackRock

"If we are to succeed in this ever-changing environment, then learning and adapting is absolutely critical. In this book, Brad Staats unpacks the science of why we don't learn at work and compellingly shows us how we can do better. A vital guide for thriving in the twenty-first century."

—**FRANCESCA GINO**, Professor of Business Administration, Harvard Business School; author, *Rebel Talent* and *Sidetracked*

"With change accelerating, the ability to learn has become the quintessential business skill. Yet most people aren't very good at it, and most company cultures subtly discourage it. Teaching people and companies to become fast, effective, and continuous learners—which Staats does compellingly in this new book—is a fundamental first step toward conquering the future."

—**ALAN MURRAY**, Chief Content Officer, Time Inc.; President, *Fortune*

"*Never Stop Learning* is the best book ever written about how you, your team, and your organization can keep learning to do better and more fulfilling work. The studies provide delightful twists, and the stories are instructive and inspiring. Staats weaves it all together to create a masterpiece that is so fun to read and so useful that you won't be able put it down. And, after you're done, you will never think about your work in quite the same way again."

—**ROBERT SUTTON**, professor, Stanford; bestselling author, *Good Boss, Bad Boss* and *Scaling Up Excellence*

NEVER STOP LEARNING

NEVER STOP LEARNING

Stay Relevant,
Reinvent Yourself,
and Thrive

BRADLEY R. STAATS

HARVARD BUSINESS REVIEW PRESS
BOSTON, MASSACHUSETTS

Copyright 2018 Bradley R. Staats
All rights reserved
Printed in the United States of America
10 9 8 7 6 5 4 3 2 1

No part of this publication may be reproduced, stored in or introduced into
a retrieval system, or transmitted, in any form, or by any means (electronic,
mechanical, photocopying, recording, or otherwise), without the prior
permission of the publisher. Requests for permission should be directed to
permissions@hbsp.harvard.edu, or mailed to Permissions, Harvard Business
School Publishing, 60 Harvard Way, Boston, Massachusetts 02163.

The web addresses referenced in this book were live and correct at the time of the
book's publication but may be subject to change.

Library of Congress cataloging-in-publication data is forthcoming

ISBN: 9781633692855
eISBN: 9781633692862

The paper used in this publication meets the requirements of the American
National Standard for Permanence of Paper for Publications and Documents
in Libraries and Archives Z39.48-1992.

For Tricia and Dave—
with you I never stop learning

Contents

NEVER
STOP
LEARNING

Chapter I

BECOMING A DYNAMIC LEARNER

Whatever we achieve inwardly
will change outer reality.

—**Otto Rank**[1]

My paternal grandfather, Preston William Staats Sr., grew up in New Braunfels, Texas, where his father owned the Candy Kitchen, a small store that sold sweets and soft drinks. Recognizing a growth opportunity when he saw one, my great-grandfather, Preston Senior's father, had secured Coca-Cola bottling rights for the region. Preston Senior worked at the plant as a child and then, when the time was right, headed forty-five miles up the road to Austin to attend the University of Texas. After college he returned to New Braunfels to run the Coke plant. My maternal grandfather, Brooks Woolford, grew up in Houston, where he worked as a credit manager for most of his adult life. My grandfathers lived outside their respective hometowns only while they served in World War II.

Contrast their experience with that of their two grandchildren—my brother, Trent, and me. We grew up in Austin, and we both went to the University of Texas at Austin for our undergraduate degrees (Hook 'em, Horns!). Trent stayed on to get his PhD in engineering and then started a company that enabled real-time monitoring of power transmission lines for electricity traders. After he sold the company, he headed to Harvard Business School to get an MBA. He stayed in Boston for the next ten years, working at startups in biotechnology, biofuels, and chemical waste reclamation.

After I graduated from UT-Austin, I went to work in investment banking at Goldman Sachs, first in New York and then in Houston. I moved to Boston to get my own MBA at Harvard Business School (HBS), and then I worked at Dell Computer in Austin, doing strategic planning, and at a venture capital firm in Tampa that focused primarily on technology and health care services. I headed back to Boston to get a doctorate at HBS and moved to Chapel Hill as a professor at the University of North Carolina's Kenan-Flagler Business School, where I've been ever since, with the exception of a year as a visiting professor at the University of Pennsylvania's Wharton School in Philadelphia.

The contrast between our grandfathers' experience and Trent's and mine is not atypical. Careers today usually involve multiple employers and often multiple industries. Data that tracks individuals over time is sparse, but a Bureau of Labor Statistics report that followed workers aged eighteen to forty-eight over the years 1978 to 2012 found that on average, workers held twelve different jobs.[2] At the end of that period, only 3.3 percent were holding the same job they'd held from age twenty-five to twenty-nine, and only

5.4 percent were holding the same job they'd held from age thirty to thirty-four. For most people, the only constant is change.

To succeed in this new environment requires continual learning—how to do existing tasks better and how to do entirely new things. If we fail to learn, we risk becoming irrelevant. We end up solving yesterday's problems too late instead of tackling tomorrow's problems before someone else does.

But we're bad at learning. Supremely bad. In fact, we're our own worst enemies. Instead of doing the things that will help us learn, we often do just the opposite. We are unwilling to take risks that might lead to failure. We obsess about outcomes while neglecting to examine carefully the process through which we achieve them. We rush to answers instead of asking questions. We want to be seen doing something— anything—so we don't step back to recharge and reflect. We follow the path that others have beaten rather than forge one of our own. We look to fix irrelevant weaknesses instead of playing to our strengths. We focus narrowly rather than draw on broad experience. We treat learning as an individual exercise and neglect the important role played by others.

That's why I've written *Never Stop Learning*: to help you learn how to learn. It presents a framework for staying relevant in a world of continual change. I will detail the processes you need to follow to become a dynamic learner and explain the behavioral science that shows why we fail to do what we need to do. I'll also offer practical, proven strategies for overcoming the challenges. You may be your own worst enemy, but you are the one person over whom you have the most control.

The Rise of the Learning Economy

Learning is so vital today that we can think of ourselves as living in a *learning economy*. We can't just be knowledge workers; we must also be learning workers. As Microsoft's CEO, Satya Nadella, has said, "Ultimately, the 'learn-it-all' will always do better than the 'know-it-all.'" Four interleaved dynamics—routinization, specialization, globalization, and individual scalability—have led us to a place where our capability to learn and then accomplish our objectives defines whether we can create an individual competitive advantage, and this determines if we can stay relevant, reinvent ourselves, and thrive.

Nonroutine Cognitive Labor

Each innovation requires new skills—a truism that stretches back to the origins of human history but was dramatically highlighted by the Industrial Revolution and over the course of the twentieth century. This is borne out by employment data. For example, in 1910 the US workforce was 32 percent agricultural, down from 65 percent in 1850, and in 2015 it was 2 percent agricultural.[3] Manufacturing employment peaked in 1953, at a total of 30 percent of the workforce.[4] The second half of the twentieth century saw a steady decline: by 2015 manufacturing jobs accounted for less than 10 percent of the total workforce.[5] The percentages look different in other parts of the world, but the dramatic shifts of workers between industries are similar.

Part of the story is that US agricultural and manufacturing jobs moved to parts of the world where labor costs were lower. In the 1800s the United States offered cheap and willing labor, so manufacturing grew, but from the 1950s on, countries such as Japan, Taiwan, and China offered lower labor costs and captured more of the manufacturing jobs.

The dominant driver of the change in employment was actually productivity improvement resulting from routinization. For example, US agricultural production more than doubled from 1948 to 2011, even as the amount of land used and the manual labor required plummeted.[6] Improvements in seeds, fertilizer, farming techniques, and technology drove the change. Farmers developed better techniques and gave more attention to managing the farming process than to simply following the same approaches to tending fields.

The same is true of manufacturing. Many decry the flight of jobs from the United States in the twenty-first century, as companies have gone looking for cheaper labor. But according to one estimate, from 2000 to 2010, only 13 percent of manufacturing job losses were due to foreign trade (i.e., jobs moving to another country), whereas 87 percent were due to productivity increases (i.e., less need for labor).[7] Ongoing improvements in technological investment and new labor and management practices can dramatically increase productivity, but they also often reduce the amount of labor required and change what workers must do.

This has important implications for the skills we will need moving forward. The value in repetitive manual labor continues to decline. Such jobs can often be automated, shifting the workforce from human to silicon, or they can be shipped to where costs are lower. Value is created when we can customize, adapt, and innovate—all of which require learning.

A look at employment data from 1983 through 2013 tells this story.[8] In the figure below, jobs are divided into categories according to how routine or cognitive they are. The number of routine jobs—such as manufacturing worker (manual) or sales professional (cognitive)—has stayed flat over time, despite the growing number of people looking for work. In contrast, nonroutine jobs are growing. This divergence occurs because learning and productivity enhancements eliminate jobs in the middle but leave lower-paying jobs (such as personal caregiving for elders) and higher-paying jobs (managers and scientists).

I have a good friend who spent her early career in charge of check processing at a bank. Her job was to supervise a workforce that opened envelopes, removed the checks, and manually entered the information. These were good jobs at the time for data entry workers, because they required computer skills that not everyone had. But employment fell

FIGURE 1-1

Change in jobs from 1983 to 2013

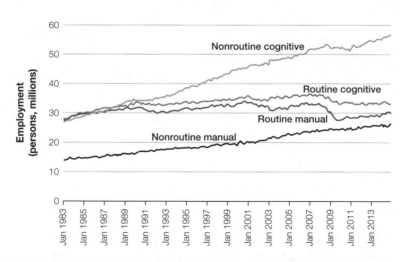

Source: M. Dvorkin, "Jobs Involving Routine Tasks Aren't Growing," Federal Reserve Bank of St. Louis, January 4, 2016, https://www.stlouisfed.org/on-the-economy/2016/january/jobs-involving-routine-tasks-arent-growing.

as the data entry process became more streamlined: checks were scanned rather than entered manually, and eventually the entire process became electronic, often with little human intervention. The workers who remained were highly trained, because they had to know how information technology and electronic processing worked and how to deal thoughtfully with exceptions. But the routine work disappeared.

Specialization

The second driver of the learning economy has been at the core of human progress for millennia: specialization. In 1776 Adam Smith began Book I of *The Wealth of Nations* by writing, "The greatest improvements in the productive powers of labour, and the greater part of the skill, dexterity, and judgment, with which it is anywhere directed, or applied, seem to have been the effects of the division of labour."[9] When work was divided so that individuals specialized in given tasks, those individuals could learn and improve dramatically. Societies prior to Smith's had gleaned this insight, of course, but the past three centuries have seen it applied ever more intensely.

As we gain deeper familiarity with an area, opportunities to learn increase. The more we learn, the more we realize what we don't know, so we invest in more learning. The cycle can go on and on.

Perhaps no field exemplifies this better than medicine. In early civilizations, it was simplistic. Absent any true understanding of human anatomy and disease mechanisms, medicine required a careful study of cause and effect to learn what remedies might lead to better outcomes.

To rectify this lack of knowledge, doctors started focusing on anatomy in the sixteenth century. In 1546 Girolamo Fracastoro posited that microorganisms such as bacteria and viruses were the actual cause of disease, and Marcus von Plenciz expanded on that theory some two hundred years later. Louis Pasteur, among others, provided enough support that the theory was widely adopted. Each advance meant that the knowledge required to be a doctor increased. As a result, it became necessary to specialize in certain bodily systems or types of care.

In 2017 the American Board of Medical Specialties recognized 37 specialties and 132 subspecialties.[10] Each requires years of training to qualify. Even for specialists it is usually impossible to know everything in a domain. According to one estimate, a physician would need to read twenty-nine hours a day to stay current with the literature.[11] Specialization requires investment, but it helps to determine where to allocate one's scarce attention.

Globalization

The third driver of the learning economy is globalization, which brings increased competition in the labor market. In the latter part of the twentieth century, numerous economies opened up their labor markets so that their workers and companies could compete globally. Brazil, Russia, India, and China led the pack, but others joined in. The software services industry in India provides a useful example.

In 1979, when IBM left India because of rules that would have required it to sell an equity stake in its operations there, few software engineers were left working in the country. Indian laws and regulations made it difficult to acquire necessary equipment and export services. But some companies carried on, either sending workers to customer locations abroad or doing work in India and then flying to Singapore or other connected hubs to upload reels of tape.

In the 1990s the Indian government recognized that the country was graduating hundreds of thousands of well-trained engineers who weren't helping its economy as much as they could; they often left the country to find work or stayed in India and took roles that failed to utilize their advanced skills. Meanwhile, technology was changing to enable remote work, and global customers were looking for solutions to their software problems. The government changed the rules so that companies could bring in the necessary technological equipment and export services with little or no tax.

These factors combined to create an explosion in the industry. Tata Consultancy Services, Infosys, Wipro Technologies, and other Indian companies grew, but then multinationals recognized the opportunity and began scaling up their own operations. For example, in 2005 IBM held its annual investors' meeting in India and announced plans to invest $6 billion over the ensuing three years in its India operations, which would result in the employment of some estimated 150,000 Indians. Figure 1-2 shows the remarkable growth of the industry over time.

Similar growth stories can be told about other countries and industries.

The implication is clear: as individuals consider their career paths, they must recognize that staying relevant means out-learning not only those immediately around them but also people around the globe. It is easier than ever for companies to contract with employees from anywhere in the world.

FIGURE 1-2

Indian IT services export revenues ($ billions)

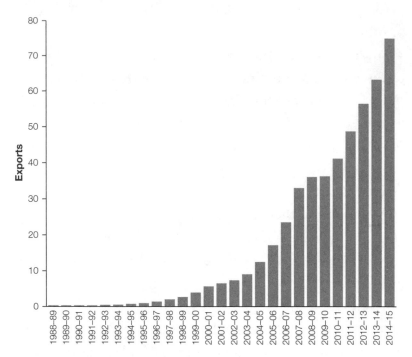

Source: R. Heeks, "Indian IT/Software Sector Statistics: 1980–2015 Time Series Data," ICT4D blog, April 28, 2015, https://ict4dblog.wordpress.com/2015/04/28/indian-itsoftware-sector-statistics-1980-2015-time-series-data/.

This lesson becomes even more important in view of the general shift in employment patterns. My grandfathers' lifetime employment was not atypical for their generation, but it's almost unheard of today. The shift is made even more dramatic by individual workers' increasing independence from companies. Whether they are drivers for Uber and Lyft or knowledge workers contracting directly or through platforms such as Upwork, Guru, and 99designs, people are competing globally more and more frequently. If you want to stay internationally competitive, you must become a dynamic learner.

Scalability

The final important driver of the learning economy is the ability to scale one's learning. Many years ago, even an excellent surgeon who stayed on the cutting edge of performance faced a limit on the demand for services. People didn't travel easily, so the expert could serve the local population but rarely beyond. As travel became easier over time, demand (and the ability to raise prices for expertise) increased. Specialization, too, was more common, because a higher income made the investment in specialized training worthwhile.

Information and communication technologies have further broken these bonds. Now one can use the internet not only to market one's services but to reach a still larger audience. The rise of information technology means that knowledge can be stored—for example, by writing software to capture supply chain management decisions or tax regulations—and then distributed. Even better, because the marginal cost of information products is close to zero (it costs little to sell a second copy once the investment has been made to produce the first one), it is economically attractive to sell one's work much more broadly than was ever possible before.

Becoming a Dynamic Learner

Staying relevant in the learning economy requires dynamic learning. Dynamic learners both share knowledge broadly and use network effects (the value of services increases as more people use them: think Facebook). Failing to learn and adapt means being left behind. This creates meaningful risk for our organizations, ourselves, and our children. It's not just knowledge that's necessary—it's using that knowledge to build more knowledge. In other words, to learn.

This is the underlying challenge that drew me to academia. As an engineer, an investment banker, and a venture capitalist, I watched intelligent, motivated people struggle to meet their objectives. Although many of them failed, I also encountered those who consistently performed at a higher level. I could not immediately see the differences—in general, these people had similar education, training, and resources. Upon reflection, I realized that some people were learning continually, and others were not.

I had identified the question—What principles lead to dynamic learning?—but I didn't know the answer. Over the past fifteen years, my research has sought that answer.

To investigate the topic of learning more deeply, I decided to situate myself between two academic fields: operations and behavioral science. I chose the former because at its core, learning is not a theoretical exercise; it's a practical one. Operations is concerned with improving outcomes. To do that means looking at operational processes—how inputs are converted into outputs—and then making them better. I use the operations toolkit to deconstruct the process of learning—understanding not only the constituent parts, but how they fit together into an overall system.

I chose behavioral science because my experience has taught me that fundamental properties of human nature affect individuals' ability to learn. Moreover, even as a recovering engineer, I recognized that a process focus divorced from an examination of the people who take part in the process would be incomplete. The epigraph that opens this chapter is correct: what goes on inside our brains can alter outer reality. In the same way, what we fail to achieve internally will alter the opportunities we have going forward.

By marrying these two approaches, I've gained a unique perspective on the topic of learning that involves three steps: First, figure out what you need to do to be a dynamic learner. Second, identify why you don't do those things. Third, understand the steps to take to overcome the challenge.

This process governs the organization of each chapter in this book. Throughout, I incorporate anecdotes for illustration and research for proper grounding in order to explain what we need to do to learn, why we don't do it, and how to overcome the challenge. In the following eight chapters I will address these key elements, which I see as necessary to becoming a dynamic learner:

- *Valuing failure*—Dynamic learners are willing to fail in order to learn.

- *Process rather than outcome*—Dynamic learners recognize that focusing on the outcome is misguided, because we don't know how we got there, whereas a process focus frees us to learn.

- *Asking questions rather than rushing to answers*—Dynamic learners recognize that "I don't know" is a fair place to start—as long as we quickly follow with a question.

- *Reflection and relaxation*—Dynamic learners fight the urge to act for the sake of acting and recognize that when the going gets tough, the tough are rested, take time to recharge, and stop to think.

- *Being yourself*—Dynamic learners don't try to conform; they're willing to stand out.

- *Playing to strengths*—Dynamic learners don't try to fix irrelevant weaknesses; they play to their strengths.

- *Specialization* and *variety*—Dynamic learners build a T-shaped portfolio of experiences—deep in one area (or more) and broad in others.

- *Learning from others*—Dynamic learners recognize that learning is not a solo exercise.

In the ensuing chapters I'll unpack each of these ideas to illustrate how to become a dynamic learner who not only stays relevant in our changing world but excels in and shapes it.

Chapter 2

WHY DON'T WE LEARN FROM FAILURE?

Oh, yes. The past can hurt. But the way I see
it, you can either run from it or learn from it.

—**Rafiki** (*The Lion King*)

Walt Disney's early years in the Midwest included getting
fired from a newspaper job for a lack of creativity and going
bankrupt because of a failed cartoon distribution deal. After
he moved to California and started an animation company,
his star character, Oswald the Lucky Rabbit, was taken from
him owing to a poorly written contract. The distributor also
hired away his animators. Despite these failures, Disney
kept moving forward: he created his most iconic character,
Mickey Mouse, and launched a new venture. (At least one
distributor thought that a large cartoon mouse would scare
moviegoers away.) Disney's setbacks led to evolution and
innovation in his cartoons, movies, television programs,
and, eventually, theme parks.

But he's an exception. Most of the time, we don't learn from our failures, even though we know we ought to. That's what makes the story of Thom Crosby, the CEO of Pal's Sudden Service, so remarkable. From his experience we can learn what it takes to make the most of our failures.

Launching a New Product at Pal's Sudden Service

Crosby looked at the weekly sales report and saw that in store after store, salads were underperforming the forecast targets. The only one that showed any promise was the cheeseburger salad. Perhaps that shouldn't have been surprising, since Pal's, a chain of twenty-eight restaurants in Tennessee and Virginia, specialized in burgers and fries. Although most Pal's restaurants offered no place for customers to sit and eat, the company had experienced more than a decade of consistent increases in same-store sales.[1]

Pal's excelled in the cutthroat quick-service industry because customers knew that it could be counted on to quickly and reliably serve a tasty meal from a straightforward menu of burgers, hot dogs, and sandwiches. During the peak time of the day, customers pulled away from Pal's drive-through windows every 18 seconds, whereas data showed that McDonald's and Taco Bell took 64 and 104 seconds, respectively. Pal's prided itself on getting *every* order correct. In 2001 this excellent quality was recognized when it became the first restaurant company to win the Malcolm Baldrige National Quality Award—a prestigious honor conferred by the US Department of Commerce.

Nevertheless, Crosby was constantly on the lookout to understand how changing consumer trends might require

Pal's to adjust to keep delighting its customers. One such trend was an interest in more-healthful eating. This could be seen both in survey data indicating a flagging interest in traditional fast food and in the proliferation of new, health-conscious competitors such as Chipotle, Panera, Sweetgreen, and B. Good. The idea of offering a line of salads at Pal's had been discussed off and on for many years. After careful consideration, Crosby and the new-product committee at Pal's decided that it might be time to offer a healthful alternative, so they came up with a new line that included several salads.

Pal's had a formal structure for evaluating introductions. First, every product had to fit the company's model on five criteria:

- *Simplicity.* Does it have four or fewer ingredients, so as not to slow down Pal's fast production model?

- *Image.* Is the product "classic American" food?

- *Price and margin.* Will the necessary price meet customers' budgets, and is the margin a fit for Pal's business model?

- *Supply chain.* Are the right suppliers available?

- *Market reception.* Is it likely that customers will buy the product?

When the committee evaluated salads, the potential performance appeared acceptable if not outstanding. Salads seemed complex to produce, and some believed that they were beyond Pal's brand image. Nevertheless, Crosby felt that the potential was sufficient to field test the product.

Pal's field tests began with a new product in one store. If the product looked promising after several months, it was moved to the next stage: a three-store trial for an additional six months. The salads' performance was again on the low side of acceptable, but still intriguing enough for Crosby to decide to proceed. The three stores chosen included one that believed in the idea, one that was neutral, and one that was opposed. The data that resulted was muddled—neither clearly good nor clearly bad. The committee recommended that salads not move forward. But Crosby overruled the committee and launched salads across the chain.

From the beginning, customer response was lukewarm. After weeks of subpar reports had come in, Crosby admitted that "it was clear our customer didn't come to Pal's for salads," so he terminated the line.[2] The experiment had cost Pal's close to half a million dollars. Crosby reflected on his decision and the process the company had followed. "I very publicly acknowledged that this one was on me. As long as it is legally, morally, ethically correct—you are allowed one mistake of any kind—just don't do it again, learn from it. I tell people that I've had a $6 million education at Pal's, given my mistakes."[3]

Although the salad launch proved a failure, subsequent launches, such as the introduction of breakfast items, were anything but. Crosby's approach to learning allowed the company to grow in sales and volume, at both the store and the chain level, for more than a decade. Furthermore, in 2015 Pal's had the industry's highest revenue per square foot—$1,100—and its return on assets, 35 percent, dwarfed that of its competitors.

Learning from failure is often treated as the equivalent of the Big Bang. A failure occurs, and the "hero" realizes what went wrong and comes up with a great discovery—as happened with Marie Curie and radium. But that is not the norm. Rather, truly learning from failure is a slog—hard, painful, and slow. Moreover, we often actively work against ourselves at every step to *not* learn. That is why Thom Crosby's salad story is so important—it demonstrates that learning from failure actually occurs. Progress is not only two steps forward, one step back, but often running in place—or backward, or sideways.

It is borderline tautological to say that we must try new things to learn. Of course we must—if we never do anything new and different, our ability to gain further knowledge will be limited at best. After getting my MBA, I spent time working at a venture capital firm. Being around early-stage companies, one can't avoid the mantra "Fail fast." The point of that advice isn't to waste investors' money but, rather, to appreciate that new ideas must be tested to see what works and what doesn't. This thinking has led the author and consultant Tom Peters to suggest that the winning strategy for organizations is WTTMSW: "Whoever tries the most stuff wins." Quickly trying new ideas helps you see which things you believed were right were actually wrong and which you didn't even know about in the first place. When we open ourselves to failure, we invite entirely new possibilities for learning.

Failure can also change how we act. The discovery that a belief we had was wrong can alter how we look for new information. We become more likely to expand both the breadth and the depth of our investigation: we might talk to someone different, and we might spend more time considering what has occurred. Since failure is to some degree a surprise, it makes us change our assumptions. We reflect on what happened and how to address it going forward. After Crosby's unsuccessful salad launch at Pal's, he stepped back to consider what had gone wrong. He had been convinced that changing market demands necessitated a response, and that salads would provide it. Knowing that he couldn't make the same mistake again if he was to practice what he preached, he spent time trying to understand what the mistake had actually been. He recognized that he needed to do a better job of listening to his new-product committee, even when the members' perspective differed from his.

Failure also changes our motivation to act. When we succeed, we're inclined, quite understandably, to stay the course. At a basic level we have some notion of how we should perform. When we meet that expectation, we have no need to change. But when we perform worse than we expected, we're forced to confront the hard reality that something is not working as expected or desired. Few venture capitalists question their approach to investment when their portfolio companies are doing well. But if companies begin to struggle, or forgone investment opportunities excel, it becomes necessary to contemplate what went wrong and how to improve the approach going forward.

Challenges in Learning from Failure

The reason we need failure to learn is straightforward: learning requires trying new things, and sometimes new things don't work as expected. Failure creates a powerful learning cocktail, mixing new ideas with novel information and a motivation to experiment. Despite that wonderful reasoning, however, I've yet to teach a class on learning from failure, give a talk on the subject, or even strike up an idle conversation about it without hearing how hard it is. I am not immune to this challenge myself, even though I research and teach learning from failure. A regular part of my life as an academic consists of sending my research out to journals in the hope that they will publish it. Acceptance rates are often below 10 percent, so rejection is common. Even knowing that I'll sometimes fail and that I will learn from it and be able to improve my work before sending it to another journal, if necessary, I still suffer a brief Pavlovian shudder when I see a decision email from a journal in my inbox.

Why is it so difficult to incorporate failure in our learning journeys? Because a focus on success leads both to a fear of failure and to an inability to see the failure that occurs around us.

Fear of Failure

Fear of failure is known as *atychiphobia*. Although few readers are likely to warrant a clinical diagnosis, research shows that almost everyone experiences this to some degree.[4] When you fail, something has gone "wrong." And wrong is painful. You can experience the pain as embarrassment, shame, or anxiety. Our bodies respond to failure as they would to other high-stress situations—the adrenal gland increases its production of the hormone cortisol.[5] Cortisol creates a boost of energy when the body needs to fight an unwanted intrusion into its controlled system, such as a disease.

The response to failure can resemble the response to physical pain. Research shows that people who have experienced a failure are likely to report feeling more pain—and to have a lower tolerance for it—than people who experience success.[6] In one set of studies, participants completed an intelligence test and were told that they had succeeded or failed. This feedback was random rather than connected to actual performance. The members of one group were told they had performed in the 90th percentile: the success condition. Those in the other group were told they had performed in the 20th percentile: the failure condition. After the feedback, each participant placed one hand in a bucket of freezing cold water. Those in the failure condition reported worse pain and removed their hands much faster than those in the success condition.

Like failure at tasks, failure in social situations is painful. Ethan Kross, a psychologist at the University of Michigan, and colleagues showed participants pictures of romantic partners who had recently broken up with them and also placed a very hot object on their forearms.[7] Using functional magnetic resonance imaging, which captures activity in the brain, the researchers found that the two experiences activated similar parts of the brain (the secondary somatosensory cortex and the dorsal posterior insula, to be precise).

Perhaps nowhere is the fear (and pain) of failure clearer than in our work lives. In most organizations failure is a serious matter. Although lip service may be given to the idea that it is valuable, in reality failure brings pain of the organizational variety: a lower budget, being passed over for a promotion, a biting remark from one's boss. It seems to throw the future into uncertainty, because we risk losing the support of the stakeholders we need to progress in our careers.

The work of Amy Edmondson, of Harvard Business School, highlights just how debilitating the fear of failure in organizations can be.[8] I had the good fortune to take a class on field research methods from her in my first year as a doctoral student. One of Edmondson's key observations was that in studying a new topic, a researcher needed to be prepared to encounter failure and to continue studying the topic doggedly. But because failure meant that an assumption was wrong, we should always look to see if it might be wrong in an interesting way. The perfect illustration of that is from Edmondson's own innovative work, which has explored how organizations can create environments in which it's safe to fail. How she ended up there is illustrative.

In an early study, Edmondson sought to correlate leadership behaviors and nursing mistakes—a reasonably simple idea that gave her an excellent start as a young researcher. She used recognized scales and had nurses fill out surveys about their leaders' good practices—Did they set direction? Did they coach? and so forth. She also collected data on the detection of errors. After cleaning and organizing the data, she ran her regression models to see how the variables were correlated. Now, we'd all like to believe that the teams of good leaders make fewer errors. If that's true, the regression should have shown a negative coefficient. But when Edmondson ran the model, it came back with a positive coefficient. Nursing teams with "better" leaders made *more* errors. Why? Well, maybe an error had been made in the coding of the data. Speaking from experience, I know that type of failure is simply a mistake. Learning can be done about how to do better data preparation, but not about the idea of interest.

In Edmondson's case, no such error had been made. The relationship was accurate. The explanation will be all too familiar to most readers: errors in health care generally require that an individual self-report the mistake. If a patient has a severe adverse reaction, or dies, the error can be clearly identified. But far more often, a nurse must admit that the mistake occurred. She may forget to do something, such as wash her hands; place the wrong medication by a bedside but recover it before it is swallowed; or put the wrong setting on the IV drip but be corrected by another caregiver. Good leaders recognized that sweeping such things under the rug did not create a safer environment. Only if the challenges were put out on the table would it be possible to learn and improve.

How We Contribute to the Fear of Failure

So far, it seems quite reasonable to at least be nervous about failure—even if it's valuable, it's still embarrassing, causes real pain, and may get us fired. But we also know—as Mark Zuckerberg, the CEO of Facebook, has said—that "in a world that is changing really quickly, the only strategy that is guaranteed to fail is not taking risks."

One reason we're afraid to take risks is that we overemphasize the possible negative outcomes. The chance of experiencing a loss can stop us dead in our tracks. Research suggests that for us to act, the possible gain must be twice as great as the risk.[9] In other words, if the risk is losing $100, we want the possible gain to be $200. The exact amount required to incentivize participation varies, but think for a second what this formula implies. Suppose a coin flip will decide the outcome. Then you would effectively be investing $100 for a 50 percent chance at $300 and a 50 percent chance at $0. That equates to an expected return of 50 percent. For less than that, many people will simply say no thanks. Unfortunately, this can be debilitating. How many of the choices we make can truly advance our cause by 50 percent in one fell swoop? If you can't rely on extravagantly advantageous conditions to aid your learning journey, what can you do?

You can begin by understanding that despite a fear of failing, people actually overestimate their future suffering (known as *impact bias*).[10] If your mother was like mine, always insisting that things would not be as bad as they seemed, she was right. Research shows that people are poor at predicting either the intensity or the duration of their feelings after a negative event such as failing at a task, losing a job, blowing an interview, flunking a test, or getting dumped by a significant other.[11]

For example, when psychologists offered individuals a gamble with a 50 percent chance of winning $5 and a 50 percent chance of losing $3, most turned down the opportunity.[12] The reason, they explained, was that they expected the pain from the loss to be much greater than the pleasure from the win. In fact, the researchers found that the degree of happiness reported in the winning group matched the degree of unhappiness reported in the losing group.

Why do things not turn out to be as bad as we fear they will? First, when we consider the future, we tend to identify bad possible outcomes more readily than good ones.[13] Research highlights how frequently bad overpowers good. Anticipating bad possibilities triggers more fear, and the cycle of inaction continues. When faced with uncertainty, we underestimate the learning benefits that may accrue from failure. For example, when Pfizer was developing its drug UK-92480, company scientists were hoping to treat spasms in the coronary arteries that caused chest pain. The trials were a failure, but the researchers discovered a side effect: patients on the drug experienced a significant increase in their interest in sexual activity, and the drug turned into a billion-dollar blockbuster: Viagra. Not all failures will generate such lucrative side effects, but attempting to understand both the challenges and the benefits of taking risks is important for learning.

We also overestimate the negative effects of failure because we don't recognize that it is a normal part of life. Psychological research shows that we commonly cycle through four steps in response to bad outcomes: attention, reaction, explanation, and adaptation.[14] First, when we fail, we are likely to notice it. Not surprisingly, research tells us that unexpected events are more likely to get our attention than expected ones, and failure is by definition unexpected. Second, we respond to the event. In the case of failure, the response is often negative—surprise, shock, embarrassment, fear. This is the step we focus on before we take a risk, and anticipating it can paralyze us. However, we don't stop there.

It is in moving to the third step, explanation, that learning occurs. When we try to understand what happened, we may see the flaw in our prior model of the world. In this step we start to look for new information and also change the process by which we look for it. In the final step, we adapt to the new information we have discovered. Adaptation can be both an emotional and a cognitive process. If we understand why we failed and how that understanding can move us forward, we can stabilize the emotions we experienced in the reaction step.

As you begin to appreciate that failure wasn't as bad as you expected and that it permits you to learn, you can shift from pain to joy. In addition, cognitive changes may occur as you implement new learned behaviors. When functioning effectively, our bodies have a built-in failure defense mechanism. Just like the immune system, that failure system responds to threatening outside agents—at least metaphorically. When we're at our best, these initially destabilizing threats focus our attention, lead to a reaction, give rise to an explanation, and result in adaptation, all with the result that we learn.

Inability to See the Failure That Occurs around Us

A comparison of the failure system to the immune system is apt not only because both can lead to improved well-being but also, unfortunately, because both are prone to predictable breakdown. A broad class of diseases, described as autoimmune, occur when the immune system mistakes healthy cells for invaders and seeks to kill them. Examples include rheumatoid arthritis, in which immune cells release an inflammation-causing chemical, synovium, in the tissue around joints; Graves' disease, in which antibodies cause the thyroid to grow and produce excessive amounts of thyroid hormone; and Guillain-Barré syndrome, in which the immune system attacks the body's central nervous system to the point where muscles can become completely unusable.

Medical science is still seeking to understand what causes the body to turn on itself. Fortunately, behavioral science has identified the causes of difficulty with the failure system. Just as a fear of failure may prevent you from even trying something new, it can lead you to deny that failure has occurred in the face of considerable evidence to the contrary. This instinct for self-preservation isn't surprising, but it is counterproductive for learning. In predictable ways, we decline to use the information that is accessible from failure. Instead of helping the learning process, the explanation and adaptation steps can get in the way. We attribute events incorrectly. Moreover, we often adjust our standards and persuade ourselves that no failure occurred rather than emotionally adapt to it.

To understand the things that happen around us, we seek to assign causal responsibility.[15] We wish to say *why* something happened. This is a vital part of learning, because if we understand the *why*, we can adapt to improve our future actions. However, we experience challenges in attributing an effect to a cause. As Richard Feynman, the Nobel Prize–winning physicist, said, "The first principle is that you must not fool yourself—and you are the easiest person to fool. So you have to be very careful about that."[16] The events occurring around us may be a function of both an individual's actions (such as preparation for a big sales meeting, or creativity in the presentation) and the situation (a competitor's new product better meets a need, or the competitor has stocked out of a product, so the customer has no choice but to buy yours).

Research has labeled our difficulty in attributing cause and effect the *fundamental attribution error.*[17] In a classic study, researchers varied the lighting on a basketball court and asked participants to make free throws. Shooters who had been randomly assigned to the dimmer court were judged less competent than those assigned to the well-lit court.[18] In other words, evaluators failed to allow for the degree of difficulty (the situation) and ascribed all responsibility to the individual.

The same challenge can be seen in numerous settings. For example, as an investment banking analyst, I helped with the firm's recruiting efforts at my alma mater. One of our first screens for candidates was grade point average. Anything much below 4.0 led to a rejection. As the group's one engineering graduate, I continually had to remind the others that our engineering applicants were in a program with a lower average GPA, and thus we should take into consideration not only major but courses taken. Research supports my experience, showing that people ascribe high grades to talent even when those grades are known to result from grade inflation.[19]

From a learning standpoint, misattribution creates an unnecessary challenge. If you don't adequately understand whether an individual or a situation was responsible for an outcome, any solution may well seem inappropriate. The problem grows even more complex when failure comes into the picture. Psychology highlights that we draw an important boundary when we consider our own failure versus that of others.[20] In considering our own, we often overweight things such as luck or the difficulty of the task and underweight our ability or effort. (We usually do just the opposite in evaluating others.) This creates a natural protection for the psyche: "It wasn't my fault—it was so hard that no one could have pulled it off" or "That's just the luck of the draw—sometimes clients don't want to buy." But that protection comes at the cost of future learning. When you assign responsibility for a failure to outside events, you negatively impact your motivation to try to learn. If you were simply unlucky, why even try to learn from it?

Research I conducted with Diwas KC and Francesca Gino shows this challenge in action in the fast-paced area of cardiac surgery.[21] Cardiac surgeons have significantly improved patients' life expectancy, thanks to their ability to repair or replace heart valves, bypass coronary arteries, and generally ameliorate damage in the cardiovascular system. Unfortunately, though, patients still die during cardiac care. In our study we tried to determine whether surgeons learned more from their own failures or from the failures of others. The fundamental attribution error would suggest that they might ascribe their own failures to bad luck or an impossible case that no one could have saved, and the mistakes of others to a failure of skill or effort that offered greater opportunity to learn. Our analysis of ten years' worth of data across seventy surgeons revealed not only that on average, they learned more from others' failure than from their own, but also that an individual's own failure led to worse future performance.

To dig deeper into this topic in another setting, Francesca Gino and I, along with Chris Myers, looked at people's actual attribution processes.[22] We conducted a series of decision-making exercises with college-educated working professionals. In the first exercise, which was online, important information for the decision was withheld from the participants but could be obtained by clicking on a link. After completing the exercise, the participants took a survey that included questions about attribution. Their responses ranged from blaming the situation for the failure ("The activity withheld information from me") to accepting responsibility ("I overlooked key information"). We found that in the second exercise, those who had internally attributed the first failure were much more likely to have learned and to perform better than those who had not.

A second problem arises when we simply don't recognize failure. Although failure can lead to self-improvement, the desire to protect one's self-image all too often gets in the way.[23] Because failure is threatening, we try to downplay its very occurrence. After a failure, we may hold our performance to a standard different from the one originally considered—that is, make a relative rather than an absolute comparison—or even change our outcome measure. The end result may be that we no longer failed at all—rather, we simply met expectations.

My experience in freshman physics is an excellent example of this challenge. Having excelled throughout high school, I expected much the same in college. I viewed myself as a top student who worked enough but could get by on raw intellect (ah, the naïveté of youth). The honors engineering program at UT-Austin opened my eyes, although it took time. As an eighteen-year-old, I anxiously awaited the return of the first physics exam, a test on which I feared I had bombed. The circled number on my exam—twenty-seven—confirmed my worst fears. As I pondered my future in engineering, and whether everything I thought about myself was wrong, the professor strode to the board and wrote the average for the class—a number several points below twenty-seven.

Objectively, I had performed above average. At the same time, my performance indicated a serious lack of physics knowledge. My test-taking skills were such that I could get adequate partial credit while understanding very little of the material. Unfortunately, shifting to a relative measure of performance enabled me to judge my performance as adequate and avoid the hard work of truly learning the material.[24]

Not only do we shift to relative comparisons to avoid the sting of failure, but we may even change the outcome measure on which we focus. For example, after being ranked lower than expected, some business schools turned their attention to performance dimensions other than those used in the rankings, such as an entrepreneurial culture.[25] Pino Audia and Sebastien Brion, at Tuck Business School and IESE Business School respectively, completed related work showing that when initial performance is worse than expected, decision makers, both in the lab and in the field, turn their attention to a secondary and favorable performance measure—say, profitability instead of revenue growth.[26]

Paul Green, Francesca Gino, and I saw the same thing when we looked at one company's yearly worker-evaluation process.[27] The company took a fairly standard 360-degree approach. First an employee completed a self-evaluation for the year; then others provided him or her with their perspectives on her performance. Who provided each review was known, and employees had some discretion over whom they asked for feedback beyond the obligatory providers.

In theory, the process helped people identify areas needing improvement—what others saw as issues, in comparison with what the employee thought. However, the process wasn't that simple. Looking across four years' worth of data and almost 6,000 reviews, we found that instead of embracing the learning opportunity from failure, employees avoided it. After receiving an evaluation lower than his or her own, an employee was likely to drop the negative-feedback provider for the next 360. Even worse, this led to lower performance the following year.

Finally, individuals not only shift the performance outcome to deny that failure has occurred but also may use counterfactual thinking. A consistent challenge in learning is the attempt to evaluate what *might* have happened. When a coach loses a close game, he may call it "a moral victory," arguing that a much bigger loss was expected. Psychological research shows that downward, counterfactual comparisons help us feel better about ourselves.[28] Moreover, they may be accurate. Maybe the company *would* have been worse off without launching that new product. Unfortunately, it's also quite possible that the new product was a bad fit for the market or cannibalized an existing, higher-margin product. By making the comparison without attempting to understand the *why* behind what happened, we deprive ourselves of the chance to learn.

Successfully Learning from Failure

Although we get in our own way, it is possible to transcend our limitations when it comes to failure and learning. The first step is to destigmatize failure, admitting that although it's a distinct possibility, it won't keep you from trying new things.

One way to destigmatize failure is to bring struggles out into the open. Research shows that sharing them with others is likely to improve performance. Xiaodong Lin-Siegler and her colleagues conducted a field experiment with high schoolers in New York.[29] A control group read about the accomplishments of great scientists, such as Albert Einstein and Marie Curie. One experimental group read about the scientists' technical difficulties (Curie, for example, endured one failed experiment after another), and a second experimental group read about their personal difficulties (Einstein, a Jew, had to flee Nazi Germany). Both experimental groups outperformed the control group at the end of a six-week grading period, and previously low-performing students saw an especially big improvement. Talking about failures, both to ourselves and to others, makes it possible to normalize the learning behavior.

Transparency about failure helps us acknowledge that everyone fails.[30] Accepting that is not the same as encouraging yourself to fail irresponsibly. Thom Crosby demanded accountability from others and himself: "As long as it is legally, morally, ethically correct—you are allowed *one* mistake of any kind—just don't do it again [italics mine]."

Destigmatizing failure also means shifting how you think about acting versus not acting. We are averse to loss, and failure always brings the possibility of loss. Instead of considering the safety of the status quo and the risk of doing things differently, consider the risk in the status quo and the safety that comes from learning new things. Identifying the uncertainties of not learning, along with the many gains to be made by trying new activities, is an absolute requirement. Ed Catmull, the cofounder of Pixar, sums it up nicely in his book, *Creativity, Inc.*, "Mistakes aren't a necessary evil. They aren't evil at all. They are an inevitable consequence of doing something new (and, as such, should be seen as valuable; without them, we'd have no originality). And yet, even as I say that embracing failure is an important part of learning, I also acknowledge that acknowledging this truth is not enough. That's because failure is painful, and our feelings about this pain tend to screw up our understanding of its worth. To disentangle the good and the bad parts of failure, we have to recognize both the reality of the pain and the benefit of the resulting growth."[31]

One way to do this is to think about your future self. What are the consequences of not trying new things? I call this the annual review test. If in one year the environment has changed (and you can be certain that it will have), what can you point to that you've done to improve yourself and your prospects? What might you regret *not* having tried? In the performance review example, would people who took an annual review test still have run from the negative feedback? Or would they have seen that the learning challenge was to change that feedback the following year by improving?

In addition to destigmatizing failure, you can use failure more effectively when it occurs—that is, take the "explain" step. You can improve the likelihood of learning from failure in several ways. One is to seek to remove ambiguity or excuses. Chris Myers, Francesca Gino, and I explored whether circumstances might encourage people to assign responsibility to themselves. We gave participants a task in which they scanned a professionally prepared red blood cell "smear" and searched for anomalies—in this case, Howell-Jolly bodies, a marker of a damaged spleen. Some people were told they'd been successful, and others were told they had failed, but half the participants were also told that the images did not always display properly on the internet browser they'd used. We found that those who were given this excuse were more likely to blame outside events (the faulty browser) for their performance and subsequently failed to improve it.

When you set goals for yourself, you can ask others to help hold you accountable—a spouse, a friend, a coworker, or even an outside service, such as stickK.com.[32] Setting a goal increases the likelihood that you'll achieve it, but you also need to specify what success entails and maybe even get an outside referee to evaluate your performance so that you don't lose improvement opportunities.

Finally, data is a powerful tool to avoid fooling oneself. As Ed Catmull has written, "Data can show things in a neutral way, which can stimulate discussion and challenge assumptions arising from personal impressions."[33] Intermountain Healthcare's approach to data and failure is instructive.[34] Intermountain is a leader in delivering efficient, high-quality health care, in part because of its use of standard processes. However, its doctors are free to deviate from those processes if they see fit. Deviation suggests that either the standard process didn't fit the situation or the doctor didn't understand that in fact it did. When a doctor deviates, people take the data to him or her to discuss what happened. The learning opportunity there is immense. Evidence of the efficacy of a treatment is difficult to argue against. If the doctor has found a better way, the data can be used to explore that as well.

Our focus on success is powerful but not insurmountable. To overcome it and learn from failure, you must begin by recognizing that failure is not typically as bad as you think it will be. Moreover, when you do fail, don't let the learning opportunity escape by attributing the cause to outside events or denying that the failure even occurred. To learn, remember that "success consists of going from failure to failure without loss of enthusiasm."[35]

Chapter 3

LEARNING REQUIRES PROCESS FOCUS, NOT OUTCOME FOCUS

Today's society wants to skip the
process. I hate that. Do the little
things right to reach the big goals.

—Tom Izzo

I have three sons who, at least for the moment, all love baseball (as does their father, as evidenced by the frequent use
of baseball examples throughout this book). I have the good
fortune to help coach each of their baseball teams, although
soon their skills and knowledge will surpass mine. Recently
my eldest son came to the plate with the bases loaded and
one out against a hard-throwing but wild pitcher. Most of
the team was either striking out or walking. He ripped a
pitch, but unfortunately it went straight to the shortstop,
who fielded it on one hop and, given how hard it was hit,
easily turned a double play from second base to first base.

My son's response was not one of grudging acceptance that he had done everything right but gotten unlucky. Rather, it was "Dad, even a weakly hit ground ball would have scored a run." Of course, no coach would send a player up for an at bat and tell him to mishit the ball in an attempt to get lucky. But after seeing what happened, that is exactly what my son was wishing for. All my sons, when evaluating their performance in a game, react this way. They tend to view how well they hit the ball as a function of whether they got on base (the outcome), not of how hard and where they hit it (more accurate measures of the process).

Unfortunately, their tendency is not uncommon. Most of the time, even though we know that learning requires evaluating the process we used to get to an outcome, we focus on the outcome instead. That's not the approach Robert Booth takes, however, and we can learn from him how a process focus leads to learning.

A Process Focus in Orthopedic Surgery

When Robert Booth began his career as an orthopedic surgeon, in the 1970s, he looked much the same as others like him.[1] He performed procedures such as hip and knee replacements and arthroscopy and provided nonsurgical care for orthopedic conditions. As time passed, though, Booth began to appreciate that if he wanted to improve the quality of outcomes for his patients, he needed a full understanding of the entire process of care—from initial meetings to surgery and through recovery. He decided to focus first on knee and hip replacements and eventually on total knee replacements only, thus increasing the number of

surgeries he performed of that type. As he grew more familiar with that procedure, he was able to identify new areas for
improvement.

Booth's model centered on completing the work quickly
in order to achieve the best possible results for his patients.
He wrote, "I once heard it said that there are three kinds of
surgeons—fast/good, fast/bad, and slow/bad—but there are
no slow/good surgeons. Clearly, the ability to operate quickly
and efficiently is a priority. At some centers, the average
operative time for a primary total knee arthroplasty (TKA)
is <30 minutes. If you observe such a procedure, what you
should focus on is the *process*, not the prosthesis . . . The
more efficient we become, the more we study that *process*, the
more skill we develop, and the better results we get [italics
added]."[2] To build an efficient and effective model, Booth
created and continually improved a process that managed
care as a system.

Booth made a number of changes in comparison with
other orthopedic practices. For preoperative care these
ranged from the relatively straightforward (for example,
he called patients personally the night before a procedure
to calm fears and decrease the no-show rate) to the more
complex: he arranged for the hospital he was working in to
provide his practice with a dedicated admissions space so
that his team could not only improve its own workings but
also avoid being interrupted by other, less-process-focused
doctors. He standardized numerous things, from each step
taken during a procedure to using a standing rather than
supine X-ray to get the exact view of a knee he wanted.

Booth and his team paid attention to aspects of the process
that other surgeons often did not. Each year they would analyze the surgical tool sets they used and remove infrequently

used tools. This saved money and time on sterilization and created space in the operating theater. The removed tools were kept in a sterile backup set in the operating room in case they were unexpectedly needed.

Booth even focused attention on the staff members in charge of sterilizing equipment. They were often among the lowest-paid people in the hospital, but he recognized that if they did not do their jobs, he wouldn't be able to operate. He brought them into the OR to show them the importance of their work and created competitions in which the people who did their work best got tickets to local sporting events. Finally, to coordinate the entire process, Booth held weekly staff meetings that not only addressed the coming week's logistics but also focused on improvement opportunities.

Booth carried his process focus into the operating room, too. Over time he decided that epidural anesthesia provided the best pain management during and after knee replacements. It took more time to deliver and was more complex, so he worked with both the anesthesiologists and the hospital to secure additional space close by.

To improve efficiency during a procedure, Booth always worked with the same team of surgical nurses; they knew what he wanted when he wanted it. He also used only one prosthesis supplier for his replacement joints. Although that meant that a device might not be perfectly tailored for an individual, differences in device-patient fit were typically quite small. This focus helped him gain additional attention from the supplier and learn the intricacies of the device. He was also able to suggest novel innovations within the prosthetics that resulted in improved quality for patients. Booth did not try to be on the cutting edge of technology. He recognized that learning within the process was most important for delivering efficient and effective care, so it was better to stick with a tried-and-true, improved approach than to jump from one new idea to the next. Finally, after finishing a procedure, Booth gave patients his phone number to comfort them and so that he would hear about any issues that arose.

Booth's focus on the process served him and his patients well. Over fifteen years he conducted more total knee replacements than any other surgeon in the United States. He was recognized four times by the Knee Society with its research award and served as its president.[3]

The case of Robert Booth illustrates the difficulty of and the opportunity from taking a process focus to learning. Each part of a system is given careful study in order to build deeper understanding. With practice, the parts improve, but so do the connections between them. In this approach, the focus isn't on the outcome—although that, too, improves, at least eventually. Process-focused learners recognize that they aren't fixed in their ability to learn. With effort and study, they can achieve significant change.

Why Does a Process Focus Lead to Learning?

Process-focused learners can be found in many places. Taichi Ohno, the creator of the Toyota Production System, which transformed Toyota Motor Company from a post–World War II afterthought into one of the world's largest and most consistently profitable automakers, is an example. Ohno knew that the system inside any organization was flawed, not because people didn't work hard but because perfect understanding of a complex situation rarely exists—and even if it does, the outside environment will change and introduce new challenges. He once said, "Having no problems is the biggest problem of all." Because all systems have flaws, seeking out those flaws and eliminating them is the only way to learn and improve. Ohno's approach to production, today known as "lean,"[4] is now used not only in manufacturing but also in industries from health care to software.[5] In one of many examples, Ohno, inspired by the cord a rider could pull to stop a trolley, installed "andon" cords on his production lines and instructed workers to pull them whenever anything went wrong in the process. Why? Because it would allow them to learn immediately what had gone amiss and how to fix it.

A process focus is also often a winning strategy in sports. After becoming the general manager and performance director for Great Britain's Team Sky (professional cycling) in 2010, Dave Brailsford was determined to make everything 1 percent better. He examined all aspects of the process—from obvious choices, such as how riders trained and ate, to less obvious ones, such as effective hand washing to avoid infection, the best pillow to take to hotels for sleeping, and the most effective massage gel.[6] Brailsford's focus paid off when his team won not only back-to-back Tours de France—the most prestigious race in cycling—but also 70 percent of the available gold medals at the 2012 Olympics. (Brailsford was the coach for the British Olympic cycling team as well.) As Nick Saban, the head football coach at Alabama, who has multiple national championships to his name, says, "When you have a system, you kind of get in a routine of what's important . . . and then you spend a lot more time on thinking of things that would make it better."[7]

Why is a process focus so central for learning? At its core, learning involves understanding what (and how) inputs affect important outputs—building a model of the way things work. Usually you need to accomplish some task— replace a knee with a prosthetic device, build a car, win a bicycle race—but to accomplish it, you need to understand the many pieces that contribute to the task *and* how they interact with one another. A process focus provides value on both fronts.

When you take time to learn the process, you recognize that it often involves more inputs than you first imagined. Booth realized that his patients' outcomes depended on him, of course, but they also depended on many other factors, including nurses, anesthesiologists, central supply workers, administrative workers, the prosthetic device chosen, and so on. The choices of the people involved were also inputs to the process. Focusing on the output rather than the process shrouds the details, and your model of the process will be incomplete.

Even when your view of the inputs is accurate, you still have to discover how they interact to produce an outcome. In some learning scenarios, this process is straightforward. For example, in the game of blackjack, the objective is to get closer to twenty-one than the dealer does without going over. (Each card is worth the number it shows except face cards, which are worth ten, and aces, which are worth one or eleven.) To begin, the dealer gives each player two cards faceup and takes one card faceup and one facedown. Each player then decides whether to "hit" (take another card) or "stay." A player who goes over twenty-one "busts" and loses. If he stays below twenty-one, the dealer "hits" up to seventeen or more points.

Blackjack can be confusing. Players make a number of choices (and some additional moves include splitting cards or doubling down). But with careful study, it is possible to completely characterize blackjack—that is, to come up with the optimal strategy for every situation in the game. After simulating the possible outcomes again and again with a computer, given what the player has and what the dealer is showing, you can decide whether hitting or staying has the best probability of winning. For example, if the dealer is showing seven and a player has sixteen (say, a six and a jack), the player should hit every time. That risks busting, but the probability of losing otherwise is too high not to hit.[8]

Although blackjack has many moving pieces, it is still possible to simulate and come up with the exact choice to make in any situation, because all the inputs (the cards) are known, as is how the inputs interact (the rules for when a dealer must hit or stay). With this complete information, one can "learn" blackjack.

If only real life were so neat and complete.

When I teach operations to my MBA students, I start with a process focus—something we call process analysis. The same was true when I was an MBA student at Harvard Business School. On the first day of class, Professor Frances Frei began unpacking the wonders that were Benihana— the Japanese-style hibachi restaurant. Admittedly, I was on edge from the day I met her. We had just been given our section assignments and the seats we would take for the entire semester. As I recall, after being introduced, Frei stepped to the middle of the room and said, "Sky deck [the last row in the classroom], I'm coming after you." She may have said something else first, but because I was sitting in the sky deck, nothing else seemed to matter. I survived that first day in part because we spent the class helping her draw a diagram of every step that Benihana followed, from when customers walked into the restaurant until they left (called a "process-flow diagram").

By understanding the process, we could see that Benihana had learned enough to create an entirely new type of dining: each step in the process built on the previous one, from the bar that served as a holding pen for batching customers at tables of eight, thus improving capacity utilization, to the order in which food was served—beginning with cheap vegetables and rice and giving very small portions of the expensive meat (although customers remembered being fed an enormous amount)—to eventually cleaning the grill with ammonia so that customers wouldn't linger and the next group could come in. Frei brought alive for us the fact that a deep process understanding had led to a better and continually improving model.

As learners focus on the process, they can see through the noise that surrounds the valuable signal. UC San Diego professor Roger Bohn studied learning in semiconductor manufacturing plants. He found that in plants that limited the noise through well-run processes, learning was more rapid.[9]

Not only does a process focus help identify relationships but it can reveal causal ones. We frequently hear "Correlation does not imply causation." It captures the point that although *a* and *b* may be related, *a* doesn't necessarily cause *b*. Tyler Vigen, of the Spurious Correlations project, has gone to great lengths to document absurd relationships that are correlational but clearly not causal (see http://www.tylervigen.com/spurious-correlations). For example, per capita cheese consumption in the United States showed a 94.7 percent correlation with the number of people who died by becoming entangled in their bedsheets from 2000 to 2009, while the marriage rate in Kentucky showed a 95.2 percent correlation with the number of people who drowned after falling out of a fishing boat from 1999 to 2010.

Fortunately, neither people who enjoy eating cheese nor Kentuckians getting married need fear for their lives. As one might imagine, these are spurious relationships. If we focus solely on outcomes, we may believe that items are related when in reality, the relationship is due to random variation or even a third factor. By carefully studying the process you wish to learn, you increase your knowledge of the causal relationships.

Professional baseball provides an excellent example of the progression in process-focused thinking. The eventual goal is to win a championship, which requires winning games. Successful teams aim to score more runs (offense) while giving up fewer runs (pitching and defense). Traditionally, baseball managers and scouts looked for hitters who could hit for average (hits divided by official at bats) and power (home runs and runs batted in, or RBIs). When Bill James and other so-called sabermetricians looked at the data, they recognized that the model was incomplete in some places and wrong in others. Yes, hitting for average is a good thing. But a hit is just one way to get on base. If a batter gets four balls, he walks and is awarded first base. A walk is almost the same as a hit, but it isn't captured in the batting average. Similarly, hitting a home run is a valuable skill, but so is hitting doubles or triples. Finally, knocking batters in to score runs is largely outside a hitter's control, because unless he hits a home run, the hitter must have someone on base to get an RBI.

Thus the core metrics used to evaluate offensive production were flawed. The sabermetricians realized that it was necessary to look at what factors truly led to runs. By focusing on the process, they could learn more precisely how to value various aspects of hitting and eventually identify where the market had mispriced players.[10]

Finally, a process focus helps build discipline in your learning objectives, even when you encounter numerous other demands on your time. John Steinbeck kept a diary while he wrote *The Grapes of Wrath*; reflecting on the writing process, he said, "In writing, habit seems to be a much stronger force than either willpower or inspiration. Consequently, there must be some little quality of fierceness until the habit pattern of a certain number of words is established. There is no possibility, in me at least, of saying, 'I'll do it if I feel like it.'"[11] A focus on the process—particularly when combined with a specific learning goal—will help you build productive habits for learning.

Challenges That Prevent a Process Focus

Given the importance to learning of a process focus, why do we often devote attention to the outcome instead? First, we incorrectly assume that the outcome provides more meaning than it actually does—that's called *outcome bias*. Second, we believe that the outcome is a reflection of our finite ability and thus we judge it as an evaluation of ourselves—so we focus on performance goals rather than learning goals, to our detriment. Let's consider each of these factors in turn.

Outcome Bias

Randomness is a general challenge in learning. Building a model, mental or otherwise, is important because it helps us distinguish signal from noise. In the absence of such a model, outcomes change how we interpret the events that occurred: if the outcome is positive, we evaluate the process as good, and vice versa. Of course, outcomes do matter. When we try new ideas and they don't work, we may want to change our perspective on the process that produced those results. Alternatively, it may be that the process was right, but we were unlucky. When we succeed, the process is likely to experience a halo effect. When we fail, we assume that the process was wrong, even if randomness was the underlying cause. As Cade Massey, a Wharton professor and a friend of mine, says, "There'd be a whole lot less drama in the world if people understood variance. Even a little bit."[12]

Incorrectly interpreting the process because of the outcome is not confined to kids playing baseball. BYU Professors Lars Lefgren, Brennan Platt, and Joseph Price examined how professional basketball coaches adjusted their strategy after close wins as opposed to close losses.[13] With a close game that finishes in a win *or* a loss, the coach has similar information: the team was roughly equal to its opponents.[14] But the researchers found that coaches were much more likely after a loss than after a win to change the starting lineup in the next game. This was true even when the team was expected to lose a game or when the loss resulted from factors outside the team's control.[15]

The challenge of outcome bias has been shown in a controlled laboratory environment as well. Rebecca Ratner and Kenneth Herbst presented subjects with a simple question: Would you rather invest a hypothetical $5,000 with a broker that has a 54 percent chance of increasing your investment by 15 percent over the next twelve months or a broker with a 43 percent chance of the same success? (No other information on risk or failure was provided.)[16] Given this limited information, the choice is obvious, but at the same time, there is a significant ex-ante chance that the broker will fail. After the participants had spent twenty minutes on other, unrelated tasks, the researchers randomly varied the investment outcome they were given—either a 15 percent increase or a 15 percent decrease—and then asked each group about the quality of their earlier decision. Those in the group that experienced a negative outcome (15 percent decrease) rated their decisions lower (4.57 out of 7) than those in the group that received positive feedback (6.33 out of 7). The two groups had the same prior information, and nothing meaningful was learned from the outcome; choosing a 54 percent chance versus a 43 percent chance at the *same* gain is undoubtedly right. Moreover, through multiple studies, the researchers found that the outcome bias was driven by negative emotional reactions. Unfortunately, after an outcome, we struggle to consider what actually happened, considering a good outcome to reflect a good process and a bad outcome to reflect a bad one.[17]

Such biased evaluation poses a fundamental challenge to learning. It's not that we should ignore the outcome, but we focus too much on it. We should learn to weight it appropriately. In fact, in settings that are overly focused on outcomes, the efforts of individuals may decrease.[18] The old saying "You are never as good as they say when you win or as bad as they say when you lose" isn't just an excuse for losers; it contains an important element of truth. Rather than judging the process through the lens of the outcome, seek to learn about the process that got you there.

Performance Mindset

The second reason we focus on outcomes is rooted in how we view intelligence. Although *The Little Engine That Could* first appeared in the early 1900s, the engine's mantra—"I think I can"—connects to research on how we learn. Stanford psychologist Carol Dweck has showed that individuals tend to hold one of two views about intelligence: that it can always be improved, known as a *growth* mindset, or that individuals are endowed with a certain fixed amount of intelligence—a *performance* mindset.[19] These views have important implications for a process focus and learning.

Your perspective on intelligence affects how you think about process and outcome. To a performance mindset, outcomes have an evaluative aspect. In other words, success or failure is a direct result of the individual's intelligence. But to a growth mindset, the outcome is simply one input about the state of the process and the individual's general learning.[20]

In a fascinating study on this topic, Claudia Mueller and Carol Dweck examined how praising intelligence rather than effort affected subjects' views of intelligence and subsequent learning behavior.[21] In multiple experiments, children received randomly assigned praise for one ("You must be smart at these problems") or the other ("You must have worked hard at these problems"). Those praised for intelligence subsequently viewed intelligence as more fixed than did those praised for effort; they also subsequently performed worse on various tasks, kept at the tasks for less time, and expressed less enjoyment in doing them.

These findings are relevant to the workplace as well as to learners in the classroom. A study of seven *Fortune* 1,000 companies showed that a growth mindset was related to happier employees; a more innovative, risk-taking culture; and better performance.[22] In ongoing work I've done with Dan Cable, Francesca Gino, Julia Lee, and Alison Wood Brooks, we examined consultants' growth mindset and subsequent work performance. We found a relationship to supervisory-rated performance and learning and also that individuals with a growth mindset were more likely to help coworkers be successful.

The second implication of a growth mindset is that our brains actually respond differently to challenges. Michigan State University professor Jason Moser and his collaborators looked at the cognitive responses of individuals according to whether or not they had a growth mindset.[23] As the participants completed tasks, the researchers measured their brain activity with electrodes attached to their heads. Those with a growth mindset actually showed greater brain activity after incorrect answers than did other subjects. In particular, they showed enhanced Pe amplitude—a brain signal that captures the conscious attention given to mistakes.[24] When we're focused on learning and the process, we don't have false confidence; rather, our brains are actively trying to learn and improve. It's as if the Little Engine was given a new power source.[25]

Successfully Learning from the Process

Fortunately, we can build a process focus in several ways. The first is focus itself. Martha Graham was named the "dancer of the century" by *Time* magazine. She was both a remarkable dancer and a renowned choreographer who invented numerous techniques. Describing process, Graham said, "Freedom to a dancer means discipline. That is what technique is for—liberation." Success, even in a novel situation such as dance, depends on understanding the building blocks. Once we understand the basics, we can deviate productively to innovate and learn.

Underlying the process approaches of Booth, Brailsford, Ohno, and Graham is the idea of deliberate practice. None of them attempted to improve the entire process at once. That would have improved nothing. Instead, they focused on small, digestible pieces. Whether you're attempting to learn how to negotiate a deal, structure a financial transaction, or hit a baseball, starting small around one piece that can be mastered in a reasonable amount of time makes it possible to focus productively on the process.

That means developing a keen eye for where value is created. Building on a process-flow diagram, Taichi Ohno tweaked the model to create a "value-stream diagram." He recognized that waste—non-value-added steps in a process—was largely socially constructed. If one didn't focus on the process, one wouldn't learn what could be removed. Toyota used process-flow diagrams to map inputs and the steps used to create outputs, but it also categorized each step as value-added or waste. A step that didn't provide value to the customer could be removed. A value-stream focus demonstrates that one cannot or should not fix everything; one should fix those areas with the highest value return.

This approach is applicable for learning in many contexts. For example, I conducted research at Wipro Technologies on its application of a Toyota-inspired approach to developing software.[26] I saw numerous teams using value-stream diagrams to understand and improve their processes. One team that was writing code for the software that runs printers realized that it was taking too many steps—literally. The test printers were on a different floor, and team members had to run back and forth—and when they made a mistake, they had to hope no one would change the settings before they returned. Another team recognized that its process for customer feedback included multiple, redundant meetings that could be consolidated. Still another realized that its basic approach to writing code was too linear instead of being iterative, so it wasn't learning rapidly enough from the mistakes it made.

Often the argument against a process focus is that it turns people into automatons. Interestingly, Frederick Taylor pointed out in his masterpiece, *Principles of Scientific Management*, that with process a worker can "use his own originality and ingenuity to make real additions to the world's knowledge, instead of reinventing things which are old."[27] The key is why we do focus on process. If it's for learning, treating the steps as building blocks that can and will change, then process is a powerful tool that can lead to improvement.

To improve a process focus, you need measures for capturing what is going on. Returning to baseball, one of the most significant shifts in sabermetrics was from discussing wins and losses to discussing the determinants of those outcomes. Early on, runs and other limited measures were considered. But measures have advanced along with technology. In 2015 Major League Baseball finished outfitting every park with the Statcast system—a combination of radar technology and high-definition cameras that permits talent evaluators to capture process metrics such as how hard a ball is hit off a bat ("exit velocity"), where in the stadium each ball goes, and the routes that defenders take to the ball. With this level of data, it becomes possible to judge the success of the process.

For example, one team, the Tampa Bay Rays, is said to focus its evaluation of players not on batting average but on exit velocity.[28]

Companies are attempting to incorporate process measures in their evaluations as well. After collecting data showing that more than half of executives found little value in their performance management techniques (which are typically outcome focused), Deloitte Consulting made its performance reviews more frequent and used more process-focused questions to move away from outcome challenges and improve learning.[29] In the same vein, General Electric has been moving away from traditional performance evaluations (including Jack Welch's famous outcome-driven approach of culling workers at the bottom each year). This change involves focus and new measures, but the process is slow; Janice Semper, an HR executive at GE, says, "Absolutely the challenge is how do you unlearn some things and how do you create new habits. We are trying to build the muscle."[30]

Early research focused on growth and fixed mindsets as enduring, individual characteristics. However, additional work revealed that a growth mindset can be taught.[31] Professors Peter Heslin, Gary Latham, and Don Vandewalle studied how managers' mindsets shaped the way they worked with their employees.[32] In multiple studies the researchers found that managers with a fixed mindset were less likely to see their employees' talents and more likely to remain anchored in their initial views. With education, their mindsets changed, with resulting performance improvement. People who learn about a growth mindset can identify opportunities to improve themselves and those who work with them. They are increasingly likely to take on challenges and to stick with them—all choices vital to learning.

The factors that push us toward a focus on outcomes are strong, but we must overcome them if we want to learn. To paraphrase Martha Graham, a process focus is the learner's freedom.

Chapter 4

ASKING QUESTIONS

The important thing is not to stop questioning.
Curiosity has its own reason for existence.

—**Albert Einstein**

Cade Massey stepped to the dais decked out in the cap and gown that identified him as possessing a PhD from the University of Chicago. Massey, an accomplished researcher and award-winning teacher, surveyed the almost 900 students who made up the entering MBA class at The Wharton School. In this august environment, it was his job to welcome them to Wharton and get their academic studies off on the right foot.

Massey did not regale them with stories of dramatic accomplishments. He did not offer them the promise of enormous salaries. Rather, he began to ask questions that even this promising group could not answer. From complex, arcane financial formulas to what might happen if they sought a networking meeting with someone they didn't know, Massey pressed the students repeatedly with questions to which the only answer was "I don't know." Eventually the 900-person audience was thunderously chanting, "I don't know" again and again.[1]

Massey sought to instill in this group of students a vital lesson: Even though we think we should know the answer to every question that arises, the opposite must be true if we want to learn. We must question the situation so that we can learn from it. When we don't, the consequences are often dramatic.

Sudden Cardiac Death and a Misdiagnosis

A properly functioning heart pumps blood throughout the body to provide oxygen and nutrients and to remove carbon dioxide and waste. It is also an extraordinarily complex organ that is prone to failure. According to one estimate, approximately four million people die each year from sudden cardiac arrest.[2] One such tragedy occurred when a previously healthy thirteen-year-old boy died in his sleep. An autopsy revealed an enlarged heart with a left ventricular wall almost double the thickness of a typical heart's.[3] Although the examination identified heart disease as the cause of death, the medical examiner did not identify the specific type of disease.

The boy's parents had another son, and out of concern for his health and that of others in the family, they consulted a cardiologist to learn why the tragic loss had occurred and whether to seek additional medical treatment. The brother's initial cardiovascular tests came back normal, but the doctor had him wear a twenty-one-day event monitor to record whether he experienced any abnormally slow or fast heartbeats.

During this time he experienced one episode of paroxysmal supraventricular tachycardia—irregular heartbeat. The cardiologist assessed this episode as a marker of heart trouble and diagnosed the boy with long QT syndrome (LQTS), a rare but dangerous condition in which the heart beats too fast and at irregular intervals, such that a person may pass out, leading to death.

LQTS requires medication or surgical installation of a defibrillator, which provides a small electrical shock to the heart to reestablish normal functioning. Having jumped to the conclusion that the brother suffered from LQTS, the cardiologist recommended and eventually implanted a defibrillator. Later, genetic testing of the brother revealed evidence of a genetic mutation, KCNQ1-V133I, which has been associated with LQTS. As a result, immediate family members were tested, and another twenty-plus were diagnosed with LQTS.

At this point the family began to question whether dramatic medical care was needed for so many family members when the initial diagnosis was based on such limited information. They turned to Michael Ackerman, a leading expert on LQTS at the Mayo Clinic, who reevaluated the data that had led to the initial diagnosis. As a first step, Ackerman and his team used a blood spot from the deceased brother for genetic testing and found that he had not suffered from the KCNQ1-V133I mutation, making LQTS an unlikely cause of death. More-careful analysis of the family's genetic tests found that the mutation many of them carried was in fact not associated with a heart disorder. Additional ECG testing of the family members also failed to reveal evidence of LQTS. Finally, further examination of the genetic tests of the deceased brother found that he had suffered from a different anomaly, one related to sudden heart failure but not to LQTS.

Not only had the original cardiologist's misdiagnosis led to a significant and unnecessary procedure for the living brother, but the defibrillator had inappropriately shocked his heart twice before Ackerman made the correct diagnosis. Ackerman noted that a simple examination of the ECG waves should have ruled out LQTS. Moreover, neither the brother's death nor one episode of an irregular heartbeat should have led immediately to LQTS. Unfortunately, misdiagnosis in medical care is not uncommon. It is estimated that approximately twelve million patients are misdiagnosed annually in the United States alone.[4]

Rushing to conclusions before asking careful questions is not limited to medicine. Rather, it is a core problem that limits learning in most settings.

Why Does Asking Questions Lead to Learning?

Asking questions to learn is not something we need to be taught—at least not initially. Young children interact with the world 70 percent to 80 percent of the time with questions.[5] Anyone who has either had a toddler or spent time around one knows that a constant barrage of *Why? Why? Why?* is the norm.

The scientific method—a basic approach to learning in all contexts—begins with a question. It helps us identify what our exploration is meant to answer. For example, Alexander Fleming was not searching for a way to prevent bacterial infections when he noticed something odd on a petri dish colonized by Staphylococcus bacteria.[6] However, when he saw that mold was growing on one dish and that no bacteria were in that area, he started asking questions. He didn't know those questions would lead to the discovery of penicillin. When we ask questions, we fill in the blanks in our own knowledge.

Several years ago, I heard Joe Kennedy, then the CEO of the online music service Pandora, illustrate this beautifully with the story of Thomas Edison and *The Great Train Robbery*. In the early twentieth century, the motion picture industry was at a crossroads—largely because there wasn't really a motion picture industry. The invention of camera technology to capture a moving picture had astounded observers in the late 1800s. After the initial shock wore off, it wasn't clear that the technology would lead to a business. In general, it was viewed as a novelty. But why watch a show in flickering black and white and without sound when one could have a more vivid experience in a live theater?

Thomas Edison recognized that if film technology was to lead to a sustainable business, the question of what film could do differently needed to be asked. In answer, the director Edwin S. Porter and his team helped create what we now think of as a motion picture. They filmed at actual locations and switched between cameras for the same scenes—close-ups and long shots—and across scenes occurring at the same time, known as crosscutting. A simple question sparked the creation of the first American action film and, through the innovation of others, an entirely new industry.

Numerous examples exist of incredible innovations that resulted from a simple question. Edwin Land's daughter asked him why she couldn't see a vacation picture right away—and he invented instant photography at his company,

Polaroid.[7] Joe Kennedy's Pandora, too, was founded on a simple question: Can music I like be used to find new music for me? With the spark of a question, learning can take us in new and sometimes exciting directions.

Finally, by asking questions, we make it easier for others to help us. As my friend and colleague Dave Hofmann likes to say, once a leader says "I think," everyone else stops thinking—or dramatically changes how he or she thinks, rather than use political capital to challenge the leader. One of the most powerful ways we can learn from others is to ask, "What do you think?" and be open to the answer.

The power of questions can be seen in the work of Karena Strella, a partner at the global executive search firm Egon Zehnder.[8] Strella spent years running executive searches for many of the world's most successful companies. She recognized that although her clients were pleased with her work, the predictive ability of Egon Zehnder's models fell short of what she wanted. Her question: How could the firm do better? To answer it, she engaged in a two-year project to build a better model. In the process, she came to appreciate that predicting future success meant not only assessing individuals' prior accomplishments but also—and even more important—finding a way to assess their potential.

Her model consisted of four elements: *insight*, the ability to take in and use information from many sources; *engagement*, the ability to connect with people to share a vision; *determination*, the ability to overcome obstacles; and *curiosity*, the ability to seek new ideas by asking questions. As she used the model, Strella found that the "supercharger" for potential was curiosity. Without curiosity, an individual's potential skills and abilities never turned into real action and improvement.

Strella's model was a commercial success for Egon Zehnder. As the firm deployed the model, it identified previously overlooked candidates—often women or underrepresented minorities—which led to an expansion of the talent pool under consideration. A curious learner herself, Strella was able to change her perspective, along with the perspective of her entire organization, and to use the new model as a key element in the company's strategic offerings.

Challenges in Learning from Asking Questions

Although children may interact with the world primarily through questions, adults do not. The same study that found that 70 percent to 80 percent of kids' dialogue consisted of questions also found that the range for adults was only 15 percent to 25 percent. Given the power that comes from asking questions, why do we so often rush to an answer?

The first explanation is understandably practical. In the words of Maverick and Goose, from the movie *Top Gun*— we have a "need for speed." Getting things done involves *answering* questions, not asking more of them. And when we're in a setting identical to one we've encountered before, this makes sense. Executing repetitive work may appear to present no opportunity for questions. Simply repeating the known solution again and again is sufficient.

Of course, this wash, rinse, repeat approach has two flaws. First, we may not understand things as well as we think we do. I learned this lesson all too well as an eleven-year-old in sixth grade. I had tested into an advanced math class. I was used to flying through tests and did so on my first test in the class. I was proud to be the first to turn in my test, and I sat at my desk feeling superior. Unfortunately, my bubble burst days later, when I got the test back with a failing grade. I had made numerous mistakes simply by rushing through the exam. After overcoming the embarrassment of having my parents sign my test, I came up with a new rule: after finishing a test, I would ask myself whether my approach had been correct, and I would never be the first to turn in an exam. This simple question—Is my approach correct?—can provide tremendous benefits in multiple contexts.

At Toyota, even in the repetitive context of automotive manufacturing, "Is my approach correct?" produces numerous process improvements. The core Toyota Production System concept of *kaizen*, or continuous learning, is based on this idea—always improve every task by a small amount every day. That requires questioning every process. The core idea—and the challenge—can be seen as far back as Ancient Greece, in the slave Aesop's fable of the tortoise and the hare. We think we need to rush through things, as the hare did, when actually we often need to slow down to go fast. Slow and steady, like the tortoise, can win the race when we ask thoughtful questions to help us learn.

Rushing to answers when the world is changing around you is a shortsighted strategy at best. The answer that worked yesterday is unlikely to be correct tomorrow. Increasingly, we are tasked with activities that require judgment and expertise—not just mindless repetition of the same answer. As Marshall Goldsmith wrote in his book by the same title, "What got you here won't get you there."[9]

We also often fail to ask questions because we self-censor, for two reasons: We think we shouldn't ask questions, or we don't realize that we need to do so. The first is easier to understand. We worry that people will think less of us when we don't know an answer. Of course, in uncertain environments it is simply unrealistic to expect to know everything that comes your way—you have to learn.

Moreover, others don't necessarily expect you'll always know the answer. Often people respect those who are inquisitive, seeing them as both unconventional and socially perceptive.[10] For example, research by Karen Huang at Harvard Business School and her coauthors has found that we like people who ask questions, because we find questioners to be more responsive.[11] This is true even in the context of dating: people who ask more questions in speed dating are more likely to get a follow-up date. Furthermore, inquisitiveness and curiosity in general have been associated with better physical and mental health.[12]

This is a key lesson I learned working with Francesca Gino, my frequent coauthor. Gino is now a full professor at Harvard Business School, and when she got tenure there, she was the youngest woman ever to do so. But we began collaborating when she was working on a postdoc and I was completing my doctorate. Her field took time to recognize her brilliance, but I like to think that I saw it immediately. What stood out for me was that in any conversation she would frequently pause and say, "Can I ask a question?"

I would be lying if I said that at first, I always found it valuable. Sometimes I was rushing to get something done and wanted to move on. As we visited companies or worked on projects together, I would think we were finished with a topic, but she would always want to ask a question. Over time, I came to appreciate that her questions were typically very insightful. And even when they didn't lead us down a new path of exploration, the very act of constantly asking questions became a ritual in our collaboration as we explored new ideas.

Self-censorship can be a constraint on questions, but an even greater one is that we often don't know what there is to ask about. The former US Secretary of Defense Donald Rumsfeld made this point eloquently in 2002, during a briefing on the situation in Afghanistan and Iraq. Responding to a question about a report that showed no evidence of a link between the Iraqi government and terrorist groups, he said, "Reports that say that something hasn't happened are always interesting to me, because as we know, there are known knowns; there are things we know we know. We also know there are known unknowns; that is to say, we know there are some things we do not know. But there are also unknown unknowns—the ones we don't know we don't know."[13]

In the immediate aftermath of Rumsfeld's comment, people seemed to think that he had misspoken to justify himself or possibly to obfuscate. But over time, more-careful analysis revealed that Rumsfeld was speaking to a truth: unknown unknowns prevent us from learning and are often our own fault.

One challenge is that we may simply not have an accurate picture of what is going on around us. A highly effective illustration of this can be seen in Daniel Simons and Christopher Chabris's selective attention test. If you haven't already seen the video, take a moment to search for "selective attention test" on YouTube or Google.[14] Once the video comes up, count the number of times the team in white passes the basketball.

I first saw the video in a doctoral class with Clay Christensen, who was seeking to open our eyes to the interesting phenomena around us. After watching it, I argued with a classmate about the exact number of passes before Christensen pointed out that I and others had missed a gorilla (not a real one, of course) walking through the scene. Yes, a gorilla. I wasn't unique: about 50 percent of observers miss the gorilla.[15] The original study of the topic, in 1979, used a woman with an open umbrella, whom 79 percent of participants failed to see.[16]

Why does this occur? Because when we focus intently on a given piece of a puzzle, we blind ourselves to other things going on around us. We don't ask why the gorilla is in the video, because we don't see it. Awareness of the challenge is a start, but only a start. Follow-up studies have revealed that if we even saw the gorilla, we are still unlikely to spot other unexpected events in subsequent videos.[17] Before discussing how to address our shortcomings in seeing things, let's explore two other ways in which we limit our questioning.

One is how we seek information. Several years ago, I was planning to attend a friend's wedding in Japan. I was going to be in India shortly beforehand for research, so I went on the travel website Expedia to find a one-way ticket from Delhi to Osaka. I was thrilled when my search returned a ticket for $350. As I prepared to buy the ticket, the carrier's name registered in my brain—Malaysian Airlines. Unfortunately, Malaysian had recently lost a plane—a suboptimal outcome for an airline. As I thought about sending that itinerary to my wife, I moved down to the next choice, China Southern Airlines, and bought that ticket at a $100 premium. In that quick switch, I was engaging in *availability bias.*

Availability bias occurs when we make decisions according to the information that is most readily available, rather than on more-complete information.[18] It keeps us from asking questions. We are unaware that additional information exists that could spark our learning. More-careful thought would have led me to assess the safety record of both airlines.

Instead of asking only "Who hasn't lost a plane recently?" I might have asked "Who has a better safety record?" or "Who does a better job of maintaining the fleet?" or "Which connecting airport is safer for travel?"

We too quickly assume that we understand a situation given the information that surrounds us. If that information doesn't suggest any alternatives or any reasons to question the initial assumption, why should we do so? As a well-meaning soul told me when I was a kid, "When you assume, you make an 'ass' out of 'u' and 'me.'" Now, it isn't clear to me how my assuming made the other person look bad, but it certainly is true that ill-thought-out assumptions are a bane of learning. As Mark Twain said, "Supposing is good, but finding out is better." Availability bias is so prevalent because we don't have time to go out and collect unlimited information on every topic that comes our way. Unfortunately, because we tend to assume that our limited information is more complete than it actually is, we end up missing learning opportunities.

The other way we limit our questioning is that even when we recognize the need to collect more information, we often do so in the worst possible way. Instead of probing for new ideas, we proceed in a way that guarantees that the information available to us will be biased. This is perhaps clearest in how we seek political news. I grew up in the deep-red state of Texas and then spent seven years in the deep-blue state of Massachusetts, so my personal experience indicates that both sides of the political aisle gather information this way. For example, Fox News has built itself into a multibillion-dollar business by answering a specific question for right-leaning viewers: "Am I right in my political viewpoint?" The network's answer is a resounding *yes*.

Data supports my observation. A study of more than ten million Facebook users found that when people look for information, they tend to confirm what they already know.[19] We drive this outcome because we have usually selected like-minded friends on Facebook, who share political news in line with our own thoughts. In addition, we are more likely to click on news stories that accord with our political views.[20] The author Bill Bishop discusses how this sorting of people who share our views has occurred more broadly in the United States over the past thirty years, as individuals have moved to live near others who see things the same way.[21] The creation of echo chambers helps explain how fake news could spread so quickly on Facebook, with potentially serious consequences. When someone has built up strong positive feelings toward a candidate (say, Donald Trump in the 2016 US presidential election) or strong negative feelings toward a candidate (say, Trump's opponent, Hillary Clinton), an article saying that the pope endorsed Trump, or that someone was murdered after agreeing to testify against Clinton, makes the partisan confident that questioning and exploration have confirmed the truth.[22]

Remember the example earlier of one company's annual review process.[23] The company had a completely transparent process: people knew the identities of those who had assessed them. We investigated how people responded when someone gave them a review that was disconfirming or worse than the individual's self-assessment, and we found that those who got negative reviews in one year were more likely to drop those reviewers for the following year than they were to drop people who had provided positive reviews. Some took other actions to lessen the impact of disconfirming feedback, such as getting additional reviewers whom they hoped would be positive when they couldn't drop the disconfirming reviewers. Overall, we found that these echo-chamber-inducing actions led to worse subsequent performance.

These cases highlight the last challenge to our questioning—*confirmation bias*. We look to confirm our existing beliefs. You can do this by choosing where to search for information—the cable news channel that will say you're right, or the yes-man who says you know what you're doing, rather than the colleague who might question your perspective. We exhibit confirmation bias when we ask questions that vary according to circumstances. For example, if you think someone is an extrovert, you might ask where he likes to go out at night, and if you think someone is an introvert, you might ask about her favorite book or where she gets takeout. The answers confirm your initial view.

Professors Mark Snyder and Julie Haugen conducted a series of experiments to show how we engage in this sort of behavioral confirmation.[24] In one study, male participants engaged in conversation with female participants whom they couldn't see. The men were shown a picture beforehand of either a conventionally attractive woman or one who was not. In both cases participants then talked to the same woman and the researchers found that the men who had seen the attractive woman interacted differently with the woman to whom they spoke and rated her as warmer and more personable than did men who had seen the other picture.

Under the influence of confirmation bias, we use differing standards for the data that comes to us, depending on whether or not we want to believe it. Anyone who has sat in a hiring meeting has probably experienced this. When a candidate whom most of the group likes (or sometimes just the leader likes) is discussed, the background and questions are subject to the standard "Can I believe this?" But when the group discusses a less interesting candidate, the conversation shifts to poking holes and the standard "Must I believe this?" In the extreme, the same quality that is a strength for the liked candidate —such as diverse experience—is a weakness for the unliked candidate, whose experience is seen as lacking focus.

The difference in how we evaluate data and ask questions is reminiscent of the US court system, in which civil courts use the preponderance of evidence as a standard (what we do when we want something to be true) and criminal courts use beyond a reasonable doubt (what we do when we want something to be false). This biased approach to interpreting and collecting data—what the researchers Max Bazerman and Dolly Chugh call *bounded awareness*—prevents us from asking good questions that can help us learn and improve.[25]

Successfully Learning to Ask Questions

If the world were static, acting without questioning would be perfectly reasonable. But we know that isn't the case, so we need to think about how to overcome the inclination to rush to answers. In his book *Walden*, Henry David Thoreau quotes the ancient philosopher Confucius: "To know that we know what we know, and that we do not know what we do not know, that is true knowledge."[26] Our goal, then, is to accomplish just this—to try to understand what we know and what we don't know. Then we can look to fill the gap.

The first step, in the words of Stanford professor Bob Sutton, is to have strong opinions, weakly held.[27] We should form strong views of how we think the world works, because they will give us a jumping-off point for learning. Once we've established an opinion, however, we should identify ways to discover what might be wrong with it and be willing to change our perspective when new information rolls in.

One way to do this is to surround yourself with talented people who hold different perspectives. If you're a leader, that means building up a team with diverse experiences whose members are willing to tell you what they think. Even for individual decisions, you can build a decision-making cabinet. Who has always told you what he or she thinks, even when it might not make you happy? You aren't looking for the family contrarian, who disagrees just to be difficult (although a devil's advocate can sometimes play a valuable role), but, rather, for someone who approaches problems differently and is thus likely to spark a connection you might not have seen yourself. By approaching that person, you not only gain insight but also compliment him or her by asking for an opinion.

Moreover, asking questions of people with different perspectives often generates new paths. For example, several years ago I was approached with an offer of a fellowship that would allow me to visit another university for a year. It was a great offer at a wonderful school with good people. I was ready to say yes, but I realized I should consider the opportunity fully. I reached out to a friend who I knew saw the world differently. After I explained the opportunity, her response was rather unexpected: she asked if I would consider visiting her school instead. I ended up spending the year at The Wharton School, all because I asked a simple question.

In addition to reaching out to others for a different perspective, you can do so with yourself.[28] Asking the simple question "Why might my perspective be wrong?" is likely to generate new insight if you truly engage with it. Working through "What do I think will happen?" "What is the best thing that could happen?" and "What is the worst thing that could happen?"—asking *Why?* the entire time—can help you challenge your perspective. As you take an outsider's perspective, you are likely to see that asking a question is not only appropriate but necessary. There may be interesting activities on the periphery, and the information closest at hand is not all that you need. All these are important steps to overcoming the limits to your perception. If you hold strong views on the basis of information you have at the moment, but you're willing to change them as you learn new things, you can be sure that you'll always be learning.

The second step is to approach problems with a *falsification mindset*. The goal in considering your actions should not be to learn "How was my initial perspective correct?" Rather, you should recognize that effective learners follow the scientific method. To do this, one looks to reject a hypothesis—that is, to discover that there is no relationship between two variables. Proving that your perspective is correct is difficult. But you can often disprove the other side of an argument. As you rule out alternatives, you start to zero in on the correct approach.

To make this point in my classes, I use a simple exercise I got from Dave Hofmann (although I'm not sure who invented it). I show the students a picture of these four cards:

I then say, "Suppose each of the cards has a number on one side and a letter on the other, and someone tells you: 'If a card has a vowel on one side, then it has an even number on the other side.' Which two cards would you need to turn over in order to decide whether the person is lying?"

The immediate answer most people choose is "E and 4." This appears to be correct, because it would confirm the basic rule: vowel on one side = even number on the other side. However, if you think carefully, you'll see the problem. You do need to flip "E," because if it has an odd number on the other side, you'll know the person is lying. But flipping "4" won't help. The rule is not that an even number on one side must have a vowel on the other. You also don't need to flip "K," because the rule says nothing about consonants. Instead you should also flip "7." Why? Because if you flip that card and find a vowel, you'll know the person is lying.[29]

When we adopt a falsification mindset, we don't just ask, "Why might my perspective be wrong?" We identify specific reasons we might be wrong and then look for support for that alternative. This differs from the habit at many organizations of coming up with a new strategic plan and then looking for all the ways it could work—for example, a retail chain that wants to roll out new, smaller stores. Identifying specific challenges, such as strong but different competitors in that market, can ensure that they won't lead to guaranteed failure—or, at a minimum, will create an opportunity to mitigate them, such as by recognizing that the price point will need to be lower and redesigning the supply chain for the new format.

The third step is to listen actively. If you think you already have the answer, you won't take the time to listen. We often encounter what Stanford psychologist Lee Ross and his coauthors have labeled the *false consensus effect*.[30] If we believe that we as a group all see the same thing, we won't pursue new answers. There's no need. Only through questions will we learn we don't all agree, which can lead to valuable knowledge from others.

To do this requires good listening practices, such as paying attention to whoever is speaking to you. If the interaction—be it one-on-one or in a larger meeting—is important enough to have, then be present. If not, skip it. Once you're there, you need to not be thinking about other topics or, even worse, showing someone how little respect you have for him or her by engaging with other things, such as your phone or computer.[31] When you're listening, interact with the speaker. Play back what you're hearing. You don't have to agree with it, but make sure that you are accurately capturing it. That will avoid misunderstandings later and will give you a clear understanding of a different perspective that may help you learn.

Finally, wait before coming to a conclusion. Especially when you talk to someone who sees the world differently than you do, you want to hear that person out and process what you hear before making a decision. Like many people, I have a natural inclination to either become defensive or lash out in a conversation when my views are challenged. I've learned, some days better than others, that in such a conversation I need to just listen to the speaker and then take some time alone to make sense of what I heard. It's helpful to recognize this type of behavior in others, too—to give them space to think about what you've said and then come back for another conversation on the topic.

We live in a world of answers. But if we want to get to answers that will increase our chances of being successful—

both now and in the future—we need to recognize our tendency to skip asking questions, or to ask the wrong questions, and instead follow Cade Massey's lead: be willing to recognize that "I don't know" is a fair place to start, and that we must quickly follow up by asking a question.

Chapter 5

LEARNING REQUIRES RECHARGING AND REFLECTION, NOT CONSTANT ACTION

The mind ought sometimes to be diverted
that it may return to better thinking.

—**Phaedrus**

Kiyotaka Serizawa's colleagues were "amazed how much he worked" at his job managing janitors who did maintenance for apartment buildings in the town of Kashiwa, Japan.[1] He frequently put in more than ninety hours a week and got so little sleep that his mother said he might stop at her house for a nap during his drive between offices. "He would lie here on this couch," she said, "and go into such a deep sleep that I would come and check on him to make sure his heart was still beating."[2] The toll on him was such that he tried to resign from his job, but his manager would not accept the resignation, and Serizawa continued to work for the company because he didn't want to create a problem for his subordinates.[3]

Matsuri Takahashi found herself in a similar position at her job in digital advertising in Tokyo. She worked so many hours without time off that she frequently ended up sleeping only two hours a night, all the while not reporting much of her overtime.[4]

Unfortunately, the toll eventually became too much for Serizawa and Takahashi, and they both committed suicide.

The Japanese even have a word for dying from working too much—*karoshi*. In 2015 the government certified 189 people as having died from *karoshi*, although experts believe that the true number may be in the thousands.[5]

The good news is that in most cases, working too long or without thinking doesn't have fatal consequences. The bad news is that an *action bias*, whereby we think we need to be always on, seriously hampers our learning.

Recharging and Reflection by Jay Dvivedi at Shinsei Bank

The Long Term Credit Bank of Japan was established in 1952 to fund the country's rebuilding of basic industries. In 1998 the LTCB collapsed with almost $40 billion in nonperforming loans. The government was forced to nationalize the bank to avoid financial catastrophe. The bank's fundamental position in the Japanese establishment made the collapse shocking, and things grew even more so when, in 2000, the government sold the bank to a US private equity firm that renamed it Shinsei—"new birth" in Japanese.[6]

The new CEO, Masamato Yashiro, set out on a bold reorganization plan. At its center was an effort to build a retail presence for the bank, essentially from scratch. That would require an entirely new IT infrastructure. Fortunately for Yashiro-san, he had a leader who he knew was up to the task. Upon taking the job, he had sought out his former chief information officer from Citibank Japan, Dhananjaya "Jay" Dvivedi. Dvivedi's mandate was straightforward: revolutionize Shinsei's IT systems, but do it fast and cheap. Dvivedi did just that. He replaced the company's costly mainframes with a server-based platform, saving $40 million in the process. He built a new ATM network with low-cost technology—for example, using multiple internet connections for redundancy rather than a much more expensive dedicated line.

This allowed Shinsei to be the first bank in Japan to offer no-fee, twenty-four-hour ATMs. Dvivedi also developed systems and processes that permitted the bank to move profitably into consumer lending. In the end, he accomplished the required transformation in one year for $55 million— 10 percent of the typical time and 25 percent of the typical cost.

To most leaders, his task would have appeared impossible. But Dvivedi was a consummate learner. He believed that the answer to any problem could be learned if he focused on understanding the core principles. He identified the key challenge and created standard processes that were elegant in their simplicity.

But Dvivedi was possessed of more than the right mindset and a focus on process. He was also contemplative. He recognized that if he was exhausted, he would be unable to understand his situation and learn. As a result, he practiced meditation and took short walks outside his office, enabling him to concentrate on his challenges. He said, "I'd learned through my career that the work was never ending. There was always another task that needed my attention. I needed to take a break and meditate or go for a walk, and then, with my head clear and my body refreshed, I could actually get more done."

Dvivedi engaged in reflection each day. He kept a learning journal in which he worked through his daily thoughts. He held short huddles with his team to discuss not only the day's activities but also the key challenges each member faced so that they could discuss and reflect together. He said, "When I came up against a problem where I didn't know what to do, I tried to take time to step back and think. And then if I was still stuck, I'd leave it and come back to it later. This usually did the trick." Dvivedi's approach to learning highlights the fact that effective learning requires contemplation.

Why Does Contemplation Lead to Learning?

Contemplation provides two things: reflection and rejuvenation. The poster child for the former is Thomas J. Watson Sr., the longtime CEO of IBM who built the company into a major global organization. The story goes that in 1911, when Watson was in a meeting with sales managers at National Cash Register, he became frustrated by the lack of good ideas among the attendees. He called them out, saying, "The trouble with every one of us is that we don't think enough . . . Knowledge is the result of thought, and thought is the keynote of success in this business or any business."[7] Watson decided that "THINK" would be the company's slogan, and when he moved to IBM, he took the slogan with him. The concept pervaded IBM's culture through the years; eventually "THINK" became an IBM trademark, and the company named its laptop the ThinkPad.

How reflection leads to learning is quite simple: thinking about what is occurring around us creates knowledge that undergirds learning. But can't we also learn by doing? If Watson's salespeople studied only sales and thought only about the sales process, wouldn't they miss the nuances involved in actually selling? Yes, they would. The learning curve—the concept that performance improves, albeit at a decreasing rate, with each additional task—is foundational to our understanding of learning and will be discussed further in chapter 8. For now let's look at how slowing down and thinking improves the way we learn.

Thinking Slow vs. Thinking Fast

Researchers propose that two systems sit beneath how we process information and therefore eventually learn.[8] The first is a rapid-fire experiential system, typically automatic and unconscious. When we've learned what to do in a given situation—how to calm an irate client, for example—we engage that routine, not stopping to think whether it actually fits the current situation. The second system is a slow, conscious, and controlled approach to processing information. If the first system quickly follows rules that we've created, the second system is where those rules are made.

This fits the learning scholar Chris Argyris's view of learning as both a single- and a double-loop process.[9] Argyris illustrates his concept with the example of a thermostat.

Single-loop learning resembles how, when the temperature varies from the current setting, the thermostat immediately responds by turning on the heating or cooling system to bring it back to the desired setting. When you engage your experiential learning system, you figure out how to use existing rules, goals, and processes to accomplish whatever task you face. That's fine as far as it goes. But, Argyris notes, to understand root causes and truly improve over time requires double-loop learning. That involves asking, "Why is the thermostat set to a given temperature?" To answer, you need to turn on your conscious, controlled approach to information processing.

This two-step view has its roots in neuroscience. Research using functional magnetic resonance imaging (fMRI) shows that the neural changes that result from experiential learning differ from those that result from reflection-driven learning.[10]

The double-loop process has two primary benefits for learning. The first is cognitive: we build knowledge. As you take time to think, you recognize things that you already know but haven't taken the time to understand. You also make connections between new ideas. Moreover, as you reflect and identify what you don't know, you can figure out strategies to fill those gaps.

The second benefit is behavioral: reflection builds self-efficacy—"the belief in one's capabilities to organize and execute the course of action required to manage prospective situations."[11] Feeling competent and capable is a basic motivation for individuals.[12] As you reflect on what you know, you recognize what knowledge you already have—and often you may discover that you know more than you thought, especially when you see the strengths and positives in your past experiences.[13]

As the tennis legend Stan Smith has said, "Experience tells you what to do; confidence allows you to do it."

To understand the impact of reflection on learning, my colleagues Giada Di Stefano, Francesca Gino, and Gary Pisano and I conducted a field experiment with a technology services organization.[14] I have to admit that when the four of us started the work, I was skeptical about what we would find. It wasn't that I thought reflection doesn't work; instead I assumed that in a real setting, people would already be reflecting—and close enough to an optimal amount that any effect we found would be minimal. But encouraging more reflection would certainly do no harm, so we crafted an intervention to observe its impact in a high-stakes, knowledge-intensive environment.

We focused on how the company prepared agents to handle voice and chat support for customers. The agents went through four weeks of technical training, at the end of which they took an examination to show technical competence. Failing the exam meant leaving the company. We began by randomly assigning 103 people to either the control group, which received the standard training, or the treatment group, which received a small intervention. At the start of the sixth day of training, the agents in the treatment group were given paper journals and asked to spend fifteen minutes at the end of the day reflecting on their learnings. We said, "Please reflect on and write about at least two key lessons. Please be as specific as possible." The participants did this for ten days. After the remainder of the training, they took their technical competence test.

We asked both groups to report how much they thought they had learned. The people in the treatment group, who had kept journals, reported a higher level of individual learning, although the difference was not statistically significant. But when we saw the test scores, we were blown away by the difference. Those who had done the reflection journaling scored 31 percent higher than the control group, even when we accounted for numerous other factors such as age, experience, and gender.

To understand why this effect occurred, we went to the lab to do an experiment in which we taught people a simple sum-to-ten task: look at a 4×3 grid and click on the two numbers that sum to ten. Identify the pair in the grid below:

8.18	9.01	3.97
5.2	4.56	9.12
0.28	2.92	6.59
1.12	6.93	9.72

The answer is 0.28 and 9.72. With practice, one gets quicker at identifying the correct pair. We randomly assigned participants to a practice condition, in which for three minutes they completed more puzzles, or a reflection condition, in which they thought about how to improve. We found that the reflection group outperformed the practice group by more than 20 percent.

In addition to taking time for reflection, you must ensure that your body is properly rested and recharged when you're trying to learn. It is easy to forget physiology when focusing on cognitive exercises. But preparing to learn does not mean merely preparing the brain. When we're rested, we can fully tap into our analytic horsepower. We are also more likely to notice the details around us, rather than fixating on a particular aspect of a problem, or perhaps missing the problem entirely. It is impossible to keep at highly demanding tasks, be they cognitive or physical, indefinitely; breaks—both within a day and across days—allow us to recover and recenter so that we can move forward in a productive manner.

Challenges That Prevent Us from Learning from Contemplation

The case for contemplation is simple but powerful, yet reflection and relaxation practices are missing from most learners' tool kits. Why? I chose to research this topic in part because of skepticism. I taught programs that included learning journals, but initially I assigned them out of obligation rather than a belief in their inherent value. As I have studied the topic and realized that we learn best by working less, I've also grown to understand why this is such a counterintuitive approach.

A simple story of soccer goalies illustrates the challenge most of us face. Michael Bar-Eli at Ben-Gurion University and his colleagues examined almost three hundred penalty kicks taken against goalies in professional competitions.[15] For a penalty kick, the ball is placed eleven meters from the goal line and centered on the goal. The goalie must stay on the line but may move left or right before the ball is kicked. When the referee blows the whistle, the attacking player runs to the ball and kicks it toward the goal. Even at the highest professional level, penalty kicks typically result in a goal. The researchers found that goalies jump to the left 49.3 percent of the time, jump to the right 44.4 percent of the time, and stay in the center 6.3 percent of the time. Kicks, however, go to the left, right, or center 32.2 percent, 28.7 percent, and 39.2 percent of the time, respectively. Thus the authors concluded that staying in the center could have stopped 33.3 percent of the kicks, whereas jumping left or right would have stopped only 14.2 percent or 12.6 percent, respectively.

If goalies are more than twice as likely to stop a kick if they just stay put, why don't they? For the same reason we don't take time to reflect or recharge: all too often we have an action bias. We would rather be seen doing something than doing nothing. Norms suggest that when work needs to be done, we need to start working. When the going gets tough, the tough get going, right? These norms are locked firmly in our heads. Dan Cable and Kim Elsbach have done fascinating research into passive face time—simply being observed in the workplace, not actually doing any work.[16] In a series of interviews and experiments, they found that being seen at work early or late led to assessments of "committed" and "dedicated."

Additional research supports the fact that many of us consider working constantly to be a measure of status. For example, Silvia Bellezza, Neeru Paharia, and Anat Keinan conducted experiments in which they found that signaling busyness—for example, by shopping with an online grocery service rather than at an actual store, or wearing a wireless Bluetooth headset rather than a pair of corded headphones— gave people higher status in the judgment of US participants.[17]

The conventional wisdom in this case (as so often elsewhere) is wrong—at least when it comes to learning. Boston University professor Erin Reid studied overwork in consultants to see how it affected performance.[18] She found that although managers penalized employees who admitted putting in less time at work, the managers could not tell the difference between those who really worked long hours and those who just said they did. She also found no difference in performance between those who worked more hours and those who worked fewer. So we return to the question: Why do we refuse to pause? Four things drive the phenomenon.

The first is regret—disappointment regarding an alternative course of action. In the soccer example, the researchers asked a sample of professional goalies about their optimal strategy for penalty kicks.[19] The majority responded that they dove rather than stayed in the center of the goal. Moreover, when they were asked why, they most often said that they would regret having a goal scored when they had stayed in the center more than having a goal scored when they had dived. In other words, they wanted to be seen to be doing something, even if that something was wrong. Given that most tasks that require our attention involve uncertainty, it is inevitable that we will sometimes make the wrong choice. Remember, even though staying in the center would more than double a goalie's chances of stopping the penalty kick, that strategy would still succeed only one-third of the time. Unfortunately, this fear of making the wrong choice prevents us from pursuing strategies that could help us both now and in the long run.

The second driver is that we confuse action with progress. In their book *The Progress Principle*, Teresa Amabile and Steven Kramer explore the powerful motivation and engagement created when people generate positive momentum in work that is meaningful to them.[20] In other words, feeling good about progress can create virtuous cycles in which small wins add up over time to a large victory. The researchers used diary studies: knowledge workers recorded what happened on a given day, and the researchers analyzed the writing for patterns, revealing that small events within the workday (not only progress but also factors such as how leaders treat workers) can have a significant impact on creativity, innovation, and learning.[21]

But our desire for progress can cut both ways. For instance, completing small but relatively unimportant tasks produces an initial positive feeling, but we then have very little to show for it. Researchers studied this in loan repayment. Imagine that you have several loans of varying sizes with differing interest rates. Rationally, you should repay the loan with the highest interest rate first, even if only partially, in order to reduce your interest expense. But the researchers found that people often chose to pay off a small, lower-interest-rate loan first to reduce the number of loans outstanding.[22] Diwas KC, Francesca Gino, Maryam Kouchaki, and I did research that shows a similar effect in emergency rooms. As doctors get busier, they are more likely to work on and discharge easier patients first in order to clear the decks. Obviously, this is often suboptimal. When it comes to learning, we frequently, and incorrectly, view action and progress as synonymous. Decoupling the two is necessary to overcome the action bias.

The third reason we don't take breaks to reflect is that we underestimate the resulting cost. This can be seen in research into the impact of workload on performance. Traditionally, researchers looking at performance assumed that the amount of work needing to be done had no impact on the rate or the quality of performance. Experience suggests that this isn't the case, so Diwas KC and Christian Terwiesch set out to show that performance does in fact change with workload.[23] In their study, health care workers sped up when they had more work to do—but the increased speed was unsustainable. If workers attempted (or were forced) to maintain this pace, performance eventually suffered dramatically. I have identified the same pattern in workers at a Japanese bank, and Stefan Scholtes of

Cambridge University's Judge School of Business and his colleagues found in a study of hospitals that the quality of outcomes suffered.[24]

Although people recognize that overwork may negatively impact *others*, they don't think it will affect them. In research I did with Hengchen Dai, Katy Milkman, and Dave Hofmann, we looked at hand-hygiene compliance in hospitals.[25] Proper hand hygiene is a key factor in preventing hospital-acquired infections, which are a leading cause of preventable deaths. We obtained radio frequency identification (RFID) data that recorded when caregivers went into hospital rooms and whether they washed their hands upon entering and leaving. We analyzed almost twenty million observations across thirty-five hospitals and found that not only did compliance fall almost nine absolute percentage points (from 59 percent to 50 percent) from the start of a shift to the end, but also that the decline was faster when caregivers had busier shifts. When I discuss these results with health care professionals, most are shocked by the size of the decrease.

Research looking at the negative effects of sleep deprivation finds similar misestimation. Only 1 percent to 3 percent of people can still function at a high level after only five or six hours of sleep. However, many people think they can. (Only 5 percent of those who believe that they would be high-functioning actually are.)[26]

We not only underestimate how working continually impedes our performance but also fail to recognize that it may fundamentally change how we approach the task itself. Boston University professor Anita Tucker has spent much of the past two decades looking at learning in health care. Her work has generated many important insights, but one of the most important, in my view, is that busy professionals engage in single-loop learning at the expense of double-loop learning. In other words, when they are busy and encounter a problem, instead of identifying the root cause and learning how to address it, they simply come up with a quick workaround.[27] This is problematic not just because they miss learning opportunities; Tucker's work also shows that, at least in health care, workarounds may create entirely new problems—such as when a nurse uses the wrong-size syringe for an injection and gives the patient the wrong amount of medication. We think it won't happen to us, but when we keep going instead of taking time to recharge and reflect, it is at a much greater cost than we realize.

The fourth driver behind the action bias is that we tend to underestimate the gains possible from following the opposite strategy. As I've mentioned, even as a scholar of learning, I was skeptical about the value of reflection, so I decided to run a study to convince myself. As it turns out, I'm not alone in my skepticism. Extending the work with Giada DiStefano, Francesca Gino, and Gary Pisano, we decided to give participants a choice. After they had completed five sum-to-ten grids, we asked them if they wanted to spend three minutes practicing the task or three minutes reflecting. More than 80 percent chose to practice rather than reflect. But when they completed ten more grids, the reflection group outperformed the practice group by more than 20 percent.

When we sit at our desks and debate whether to take that short walk for a break or to brainstorm for five minutes on the problem at hand, we may think that the time not acting won't help much, even though it often does. In another study, Pradeep Pendem, Paul Green, Francesca Gino, and I looked at the impact of unexpected breaks on workers' performance.[28]

Our setting was unique: tomato fields. Here workers drive large harvesters to gather ripe tomatoes. An oscillating clipper on the front of each machine cuts the plants from the roots; then the tomatoes and dirt and vines pass through a series of conveyors, opto-electronic sensors, and hand sorting before the tomatoes are dumped into a waiting trailer. Sometimes the trailers are delayed, so the harvester operators get a short break. An unexpected break is fantastic for researchers, because we can look for causal effects. We found that a break of perhaps five minutes could improve workers' productivity by more than 10 percent. We repeated our analyses in the lab, providing participants with short, unexpected breaks, and again finding meaningful performance differences.

Successfully Contemplating to Learn

How can you ensure that you follow Phaedrus's advice to divert the mind for better thinking? You can use five strategies. The first is to block out time for thinking. Describing his sales force, Thomas Watson Sr. said, "We don't get paid for working with our feet—we get paid for working with our heads."[29] However, most people's calendars provide ample evidence of time set aside for their feet, at least metaphorically, as they rush from task to task. Early in my career, I was advised to determine what time of day I did my best thinking and to block out multiple hours at that point for writing. For me it's the morning, so now "Writing" starts the day in my calendar. I can't always protect that time; sometimes important meetings or classes get in the way. But because the time is blocked out, I must actively choose to disregard it. As a leader, you can encourage the people you work with to do the same—and then respect the time they have blocked out.

For example, Tommy Hilfiger and other organizations have created no-meeting Fridays to give workers time to think and get their work done.

Jon Jachimowicz, Julia Lee, Francesca Gino, Jochen Menges, and I investigated whether reflection before the day starts, rather than at the end, positively affects performance. We knew that on average, people were not thinking enough at work and that most people don't like their commutes. So we decided to see if we could address both challenges at the same time.

After preliminary studies, we recruited six hundred full-time employees who commuted at least fifteen minutes to work. Over the next four weeks, we surveyed them daily with short questionnaires. At the two-week mark, we randomly assigned them to one of three conditions: a control group, an enjoyment group, or a reflection group. We changed nothing for the control group and asked the enjoyment group to do something enjoyable during their commutes. The reflection group received the following text each day during weeks three and four:

> "We are interested in how people spend time during
> their commute to work. Many people find it helpful
> to focus on making a plan of their workday or week
> ahead and reflect on how these plans will help them
> achieve their personal and career goals. We would like
> to invite you to do that during your commute, too. Ask
> yourself, for example, what are the strategies you have
> for the week to be productive? What steps can you
> take today and during this week to get closer to your
> work goals, as well as your personal and career goals?
> Please use your commuting time to focus on your
> goals and make plans about what to do."

We then surveyed the groups again. We found that the members of the reflection group improved their work outcomes and reduced the negative impact of their commutes. Moreover, other research shows that continually reflecting on performance is beneficial not only for individuals but also for teams.[30] The goal is to aid learning by making reflection a regular and ongoing part of your work. Taking time to engage your slow, thoughtful information-processing system is a powerful way to spark double-loop learning.

Sometimes people resist taking time to reflect, suggesting that their minds may wander or they may get bored. My answer to that is *Yes!* When we are bored and let our minds wander, we tend to be more creative. I try to always have a pad of paper with me when I head to meetings or group events, because I'm often at my most creative when the topic has moved away from me and I'm left alone with my thoughts. Research supports this perspective, finding that boredom can lead to creativity.[31] So give your reflection time some guidance, but if it gets away from you on a given day, just let it go and see what happens.

The second strategy is to incorporate premortems for your most important decisions. The psychologist Gary Klein devised this idea as he sought to understand how to get project teams to dig deeper and learn to increase their likelihood of success. Klein and his colleagues found that when team members imagined that their project was already over, they improved their ability to identify possible outcomes by 30 percent.[32] Building on this finding, Klein created the idea of a premortem. In a postmortem, a medical professional examines a dead body to understand the cause of death. In a premortem, an individual or a team asks, "If it's twelve months from now and I (or we) have failed spectacularly, what happened?" This technique not only forces you to think carefully about a topic but also opens you up to the possibility that things can go wrong, and so leads to more creative ideas. A premortem may also help you avoid over-confidence and the assumption that your ideas can only succeed. It spurs the learning process before you begin the actual work.

The third strategy is to conduct an after-action review (AAR). In this case, reflection creates an opportunity to learn from what happened to improve future work. AARs are common practice in diverse fields around the world, ranging from the military to technology to health care to entertainment.[33] By scheduling regular reviews, you build reflection into the work process.

AARs start by comparing what actually happened with what was expected to identify either positive or negative deviations. To have a successful AAR, it is important to keep the goal—learning—in mind. That may mean turning to an outsider to facilitate the group discussion—thus helping to avoid blame—or involving a friend or a colleague if you're considering only your own activities. Next, get a complete view of what happened (or didn't happen) with the work. That means collecting information and perspectives from others, not limiting yourself to your own. Use your questioning skills to dig in and understand the root causes of the various outcomes. Finally, look to identify improved practices for the future. As a part of that process, be sure to think broadly. Yes, small steps need to be addressed in the single-loop learning category, but engage in double-loop learning to address the root causes identified and consider entirely new approaches to the work. How might you do it if you could start all over?

The fourth strategy is to have a plan for taking breaks. You need to take sufficient time to rejuvenate during the workday, between workdays, and on vacations if you are to position yourself to learn successfully. Research has attempted to identify optimal schedules for the workday, and you will see recommendations for taking a break every twenty-five or fifty-two or ninety minutes.[34] These findings are typically situation specific. It is unlikely that one length of time between breaks will be right for everyone—or even right for the same person all the time. What is important to recognize is that as your work grows more intense, the time between breaks should shorten. The other key is to think about how to ensure you take the break. Francesco Cirillo's Pomodoro Technique—using a kitchen timer set at twenty-five minutes—is an extreme but sometimes effective approach to enforcement.[35] Know that your brain is working against you when it comes to breaks, so use your calendar, a colleague, or even a kitchen timer to help.

As you incorporate breaks into the workday, you need to make sure they provide you an opportunity to recharge. A break to address a discipline problem for your child at school is not the right kind. Overwhelmingly, the evidence tells us to incorporate movement and, if possible, time outside when we break.[36] We may think that going on Facebook or catching up on Twitter is restful, but it rarely is. We distract ourselves, which can sometimes be useful, but we don't get a chance to recharge and rejuvenate. Getting up and walking around is a great beginning. Even better, go to a colleague's office or go outside for a quick walk. I find pulling away the hardest part, but I always feel better and more alive after I take a quick turn around campus or stick my head in for a brief chat with a friend.

In addition to incorporating breaks within the workday, make sure that the time after work is both rejuvenating and restful. Do something you like, even if only briefly. Give your brain a rest by working out or playing a sport; research shows that regular exercise may increase the size of the hippocampus, the area of the brain that helps you learn.[37] Read a book, or have a casual conversation with a friend. The harder your day has been, the more recharging you need. In the hand-hygiene study mentioned earlier, we found that when caregivers had more-intense workdays, they needed more time off to recover and return to their normal compliance levels.[38] Finally, make sure that you get enough sleep. Ariana Huffington is in the forefront in explaining why sleep is so important for productivity, learning, and health.[39] Recognize that in many cases, the best thing you can do to learn is not to keep working but, rather, to go to bed and tackle the challenge in the morning.

The fifth and last strategy is to vacation. Getting time away from work is important for avoiding burnout, recovering energy, and clearing the mind for future learning. A study found that on average, Americans get eighteen days of vacation but take only sixteen of them.[40] How often to take a vacation, how long to make it, and where to go all have highly individualized answers. The general advice for the first two questions is more than you think and longer than you think. With respect to the third, it is important to take vacations that let you escape. For some people that will always be one type. For many others, it will evolve with the demands of life. Before we had kids, my wife and I would go to a beach when we were completely exhausted or visit other countries when we felt energetic. When our children were young, work was cognitively fatiguing and caring for three boys was even more tiring. Our family escape at that time was going to Disney World. I liked Mickey well enough, though I wouldn't call myself a Disneyphile; but at Disney everything was taken care of, and the weather was warm, and that helped recharge me completely. Now, with the family in a different stage, our vacations have moved to more-active destinations. Avoid vacations that make you feel you need to take a vacation when you return; find those that will permit you to escape.

To more effectively use time for learning, focus on the end, not the means, when it comes to time management.[41] By that I don't mean ignore process; chapter 3 makes the argument for why process is vital to learning. What I mean is that whether you are leading others or just yourself, you shouldn't confuse action with progress. Recognize that you (and others) may need to structure time in different ways. For example, Stanford's Nick Bloom and his colleagues found that call-center workers were more productive when they could telecommute and thus weren't restricted by office norms.[42] Don't judge the time strategies of others if they support their learning objectives.

And here's an important caveat regarding scheduling: blocking out time for various activities is important and helpful, but learning doesn't necessarily proceed in such a tightly controlled manner. As much as you might like to schedule time for learning and then have the answer at the end of it, you need some slack or downtime for reflection and thinking, because it may take longer than you wish. Not every idea is immediately useful, but taking time to let thoughts percolate is valuable.

Writing this book has been a wonderful, albeit sometimes frustrating, example of this process. The book draws on work I've been doing for the past ten-plus years, but trying to understand how the pieces fit together and how to construct the narrative has been a learning process for me. I have responsibly and consistently set aside time to do the work. But sometimes I don't control my schedule, and writing time slips—such as when I'm teaching from 8:00 to 3:20 on a Tuesday. The productivity-seeking side of my brain gets frustrated at the lost opportunity. But I've found that when I do return to the work, I always have a better view of where things should go. I may not have the answer, but I see progress. So schedule your time in a productive manner, but fight the expectation that learning will always proceed linearly.

Busyness by itself doesn't lead to learning. During a meeting with my mentor, Dave Upton, many years ago, I was rushing through my to-do list, trying to share everything I had done and everything I was working on. I have a tendency to talk fast when I get nervous, and this day I was flying a mile a minute. When I took a rare breath, Dave held up a hand to get me to pause. He waited a couple of seconds, looked me in the eye, and gave me one of the best pieces of advice I have ever received: "Brad, don't avoid thinking by being busy." So fight the urge to act for its own sake and instead recognize that when the going gets tough, the tough are rested, take time to recharge, and stop and think.

BEING YOURSELF TO LEARN

> I am sorry to say that Peter was not very well during the evening.
>
> His mother put him to bed, and made some camomile tea; and she gave a dose of it to Peter!
>
> "One table-spoonful to be taken at bed-time."
>
> But Flopsy, Mopsy, and Cotton-tail had bread and milk and blackberries for supper.
>
> —**Beatrix Potter,** *The Tale of Peter Rabbit*

In the children's tale *Peter Rabbit*, Peter's mother warns him and his sisters to stay away from Mr. McGregor's garden.[1] She then heads out to the bakery as Peter's three sisters, Flopsy, Mopsy, and Cotton-tail, who, we are told, are "good little bunnies," head off to collect blackberries. Peter, the rebel, goes to Mr. McGregor's garden, where adventure ensues. He eventually escapes but loses his new jacket. On returning home, he is given medicine and sent to bed while his three rule-following sisters are rewarded with bread, milk, and blackberries.

We're taught the lesson of *Peter Rabbit* repeatedly, not only during our young lives but also as we get older and join organizations for work: fit in and follow the rules. By being "good little bunnies" who follow the norms and rules of others, we conform and meet expectations. We see benefits from this, both in how others treat us and in the lowering of our own stress and anxiety—thus we may view it as a win-win. But although we think we need to act like others, doing so can limit our ability to learn.

In her first job after graduating from Harvard University, Leila Janah chose to follow a typical Harvard undergraduate's route—she went to work for a management consulting firm. Before that, her path had been anything but typical. As a seventeen-year-old, Janah won a scholarship that permitted her to teach English to young students in Ghana. The experience opened her eyes to the immense challenges of development in a third-world country. During her visit she saw a talented and energetic people; describing the visit, she said, "I left Ghana wondering how a country so rich in human capacity could be so poor."[2] As a teenager, she knew that someday she would help address this imbalance, though she was not sure how.

To learn how, she studied economic development as an undergraduate. She focused on Africa and took a year off to work at the World Bank, helping with the fight against global poverty. Although she found the efforts of the organization well-intentioned, she didn't understand why it wasn't exploring different approaches, because many of its initiatives made only limited progress. Believing that the standard nonprofit model was unlikely to address the problems she sought to solve, she decided to move into the for-profit world.

During her time in consulting, she felt like a misfit. The work was intellectually stimulating, but it lacked social impact. Janah found herself at a crossroads. She had a job that many people envied, but she knew she couldn't accomplish her true goals there. She'd learned that nonprofit approaches had limited impact and for-profit organizations were typically unwilling to address the problems she was interested in. She decided to make a leap into the unknown. She quit her job and took a position as a visiting scholar in the Program for Global Justice at Stanford University.

She realized that a promising answer to her question— How can I meaningfully reduce global poverty?—came in pieces from the diverse experiences she'd had. She decided that if she could connect developing-market workers with developed-market work, she could address what she thought of as "the greatest ethical battle of our time: disparity in access to opportunity to work."[3]

Janah launched a company named Samasource. (*Sama* means "equal" in Sanskrit.) The concept was simple: contract with leading companies such as Google, Yelp, and Getty Images for digital work, such as confirming addresses for restaurants or tagging pictures with the names of celebrities, and then source the work in a developing market such as Ghana, Kenya, or India, taking advantage of internet-connected computers. Donations and grants would provide the seed and growth capital for the company, while profits would fund ongoing operations.

If the idea was simple, the execution proved anything but. Janah had to persuade major corporations to engage in such activity, funders to provide large amounts of capital for a new model, and employees to work for a nonprofit instead of the next Google or Facebook. The company also had to set up delivery networks in the developing countries and train new workers—an enormous learning task.

Through it all, Janah carved her own unique, authentic path, as her experiences and curiosity pushed the organization into new areas. By 2016 she had sourced millions of dollars' worth of work to developing countries and had had a positive impact on thousands of workers and tens of thousands of dependents. Building on her success, she launched initiatives to target disadvantaged workers in the United States along with LXMI, a luxury beauty brand that sources rare inputs from women in developing markets and sells its products both online and in Sephora stores.[4]

By being true to herself and forging her own path, Janah began and continues on a remarkable learning journey. Instead of following the rules, like Flopsy, Mopsy, and Cotton-tail, she embraced her inner Peter Rabbit. When it comes to learning, this is exactly right (even if we are dosed with foul-tasting medicine and sent to bed). Being yourself leads to learning.

Why Does Being Yourself Lead to Learning?

This is so for two primary reasons. The first involves motivation: when we are truly ourselves, we are more likely to expend the necessary effort. We do things for both intrinsic and extrinsic reasons. As seen in the work of Frederick Taylor, in the late 1800s, and of many others since, extrinsic rewards, such as pay, can certainly work—especially when people are earning little, engaging in repetitive tasks, or needing to use their hands only, not their heads.[5] But what happens when a manager can't clearly specify goals and create an incentive plan? Or wants to engage workers' heads as well as their hands, because learning is necessary? Today, not only do we need to learn, but talented people can work at any number of organizations that pay comparable salaries. What are we to do?

This is where intrinsic motivation comes in. Daniel Pink's excellent book *Drive* illuminated how internal elements such as mastery, autonomy, and purpose can improve motivation. When teaching on the topic, I also like to use an article from several decades earlier—Frederick Herzberg's "One More Time: How Do You Motivate Employees?"[6] Much of Herzberg's research was anecdotal, based on his two decades of experience working with companies, but subsequent research has shown that his anecdotes are grounded in how we actually function. I tell my students that if they can keep only one article from business school with them for the rest of their careers, this should be it.

Herzberg presents the simple case that the factors driving satisfaction in an activity are different from those driving dissatisfaction. What he calls "hygiene" factors—safety, pay, status—determine dissatisfaction. If we are dissatisfied with an activity, we will do less of it, or perhaps actually leave the company. But adjusting all those things so that a worker is not *dis*satisfied will fail to make the worker satisfied and motivated. Satisfaction and dissatisfaction are not opposite sides of the coin. To be satisfied, we need motivational factors that include task achievement, responsibility, and growth. Those make people more likely to engage with their work, such that they will work longer and harder and learn more.

Herzberg goes so far as to argue that incentives are more motivating to the person who designed them than they are to workers. I love his story of dog training to illustrate the point:

> I have a year-old schnauzer. When it was a small puppy and I wanted it to move, I kicked it in the rear and it moved. Now that I have finished its obedience training, I hold up a dog biscuit when I want the schnauzer to move. In this instance, who is motivated—I or the dog? The dog wants the biscuit, but it is I who want it to move. Again, I am the one who is motivated, and the dog is the one who moves.[7]

So what does all this mean for learning? To learn and improve in the long run, we must be motivated. Are we more likely to be motivated when we do what others tell us or when we behave as ourselves? In the former case, we are the dog who responds to the biscuit to follow another's motivation. When we are ourselves, the likelihood increases that we're willing to put forth the effort required to learn.

The second reason involves the process of learning. Being yourself and acting authentically gives rise to positive emotions.[8] These emotions reshape the learning process. UNC psychologist Barbara Fredrickson has labeled this model "broaden-and-build."[9] As Fredrickson explains, positive emotions did not initially appear to researchers to have an evolutionary purpose, whereas fear and anxiety clearly did. Our predecessors lived in an environment where dangerous situations were common. Imagine a Neanderthal encountering a saber-toothed tiger: he would feel no joy or inspiration but only fear and anxiety, which focus the mind and spark single-loop learning and problem solving. Creative thinking about long-term strategies would be foolhardy when danger literally stared him in the face.

What role, then, do positive emotions play? Fredrickson first hypothesized that they were important in evolution. Positive emotions occur in a safe space, which encourages us to think more broadly and diversely than we might if we were under immediate threat. We are more likely to see disparate connections and to approach things in novel ways. Research supports this view, finding that positive emotions expand our awareness of situational factors. For example, our reaction time to diverse stimuli improves, we search an environment more broadly with our eyes, and we even draw on different cognitive resources.[10] And positivity builds as well as broadens. Using randomized, controlled experiments, Fredrickson and others have shown that positivity leads to improved learning and understanding and to better relationships with others.[11]

When you are yourself, rather than simply imitating others, your learning is likely to improve. You have greater motivation to learn, and you may also follow a changed process that can help you learn new and different things. Unfortunately, it is a struggle to be yourself rather than conform to others' expectations.

The Difficulty of Being Ourselves

Acting authentically positions us to learn, but we face both conscious and unconscious barriers. For example, we often believe that our authentic selves aren't up to the task—even when presented with significant evidence of our high performance.

The psychologists Pauline Clance and Suzanne Imes named this the *impostor phenomenon*.[12] Even extremely accomplished people question their abilities and doubt themselves. The poet and author Maya Angelou, a recipient of the National Medal of Arts and the Presidential Medal of Freedom, told the *New York Times*, "I have written eleven books, but each time I think, 'Uh-oh, they're going to find out now. I've run a game on everybody, and they're going to find me out.'"[13] A survey of CEOs found that their biggest fear was that they might be revealed to be incompetent—even though they had risen to the top of their companies.[14]

So the fear is widespread. But how does it change our behavior? All too often, instead of seeing it as simply a normal part of daily functioning, working in challenging circumstances can make us doubt the choices we make. Sometimes we may become paralyzed, but often we attempt to take on the guise of someone else. The impostor phenomenon makes us act like others who, at least to our eyes, have what is necessary to get the job done.

When I teach this idea, I sometimes get questions on this last point. The impostor phenomenon resonates with my students because we all question our abilities at times. However, when I note that we are remarkably susceptible to the behaviors of others and are likely to conform, some claim that wouldn't happen to them. Research refutes their claim, but the best refutation I've seen is a clip from a 1962 episode of *Candid Camera* called "Face the Rear," in which the camera shows people in an elevator.[15] As the narrator describes what is happening, a group of *Candid Camera* confederates shift positions to face the rear of the elevator. The unknowing bystanders shift with them. By the end of the clip, the confederates have gotten one victim to take off his hat and then eventually put it back on. When we are uncomfortable and doubting ourselves, we typically seek to fit in.

Obviously, conformity goes beyond the bounds of a 1960s TV show. Joining a new company provides an excellent illustration. At first we're not sure how to act. What are the expectations, the rules, the norms? When entering such a situation, we try to blend in. For example, my first job after college was at Goldman Sachs. On the first day, I naturally felt like an impostor. As an engineering major in college, I had not experienced the traditional investment banking recruitment. As a result, although I knew the job was highly sought after, I didn't appreciate the selectivity. (I believe that my getting into Harvard was statistically more likely than my ending up at Goldman out of the University of Texas.) As my start date approached, and I learned from more people about the heady company I'd be keeping, I became terrified. How would I fit in when I got there? Not knowing what to do, I put on my gray pinstripe suit and power tie and tried to talk like the people around me ("At the end of the day, an apples-to-apples comparison would suggest that the synergies underlying the deal will create a win-win opportunity for everyone"). My wife saw through my attempt to dress and talk my way past my skittishness and reminded me that Goldman's people had hired me for a reason—they thought I could learn to do the job. And she was right. As I poured myself into the actual work to be done, I found that I could hold my own and that I enjoyed it.

When you suppress your identity to act like others, not only do you miss out on learning opportunities directly but you may harm yourself subconsciously. Research shows that suppressing one's identity can be psychologically depleting and can lead to cardiovascular disease and other health problems as well.[16] It causes anxiety and other negative emotions, which affect our learning in two important ways. First, although some anxiety may be useful, too much is debilitating. We have difficulty making decisions or, possibly, doing much of anything. This is known as the Yerkes-Dodson Law.[17] At low levels, anxiety helps us focus—it warns us that something is wrong and we'd better deal with it. During a discussion in a class I was recently teaching, one student said that he thought fear was the greatest motivator to learn. To some extent he was correct. When we're afraid of what might happen if we don't learn, we're highly motivated to work. But there's a second piece to the puzzle.

Anxiety also changes how we learn. Just as positive emotions lead to the broaden-and-build model, negative emotions lead to their own learning model. Anxiety and fear signal trouble. The human body responds by switching to fight-or-flight mode, quickly evaluating the nearby information and making a decision. Limiting the information you consider and rapidly deciding what to do makes sense if the alternative is being eaten.

But the same response does just the opposite of helping us learn. Even absent the need for an immediate decision, anxiety and fear lead us to consider fewer options less carefully and to remain wedded to our existing positions, even when we should change.[18] So the other half of the Yerkes-Dodson Law is that although low levels of anxiety may improve performance, high levels worsen it. For example, during his dissertation work at Harvard Business School, Clark Gilbert studied newspaper companies and their responses to the threat posed by the rise of the internet. We now take for granted that we can get our news over the internet, but it was not always clear how this technological disruption would change the industry. Newspaper companies had to consider not only the distribution question but also how to respond to the disruption of their lucrative advertising and classifieds businesses. Gilbert found that when people viewed the internet as more of a threat, they were more likely to spend money to respond—but they did so in a much narrower way. Although fear motivated them to try to learn, perversely it limited their ability to do so successfully.

Successfully Being Ourselves to Learn

If being yourself helps you learn, but you often prevent yourself from doing so, what are you to do?

First you need to discover how to release your inner Peter Rabbit—to free yourself to be you, within the confines of your daily activities. Even a small nudge can have a big impact. One of my research projects directly addressed this question—in terms of both my experience and the findings.

A number of years ago, I was spending the day with Wipro BPO (business process outsourcing) just outside Delhi. As the name would suggest, the company, which has tens of thousands of employees, completes back-office work for customers—such as taking calls and completing paperwork—from its global facilities. I had worked with Wipro on learning and improvement research projects for many years, and one of my earliest contacts, Devender Malhotra, had become its chief quality officer. Malhotra had invited me to meet with people across the company to see whether we might find a way to collaborate in that business. At the end of a wonderful day during which I had been introduced to lots of fascinating people and projects, he and

I sat down together. As our meeting was wrapping up and I was preparing to go, I asked him if he had any questions for me. Malhotra is quiet and thoughtful, and he paused to consider the question before replying that he would like to know if I had ideas for reducing employee attrition.

As he waited expectantly for an answer, the impostor phenomenon raged within me. I had spent the day as an honored visitor from a US university and had felt knowledgeable throughout. Now, at the very end of the day, I was flummoxed. I should not have been surprised by his question. Employee attrition is quite high across the Indian BPO industry—estimates of 50 percent to 75 percent annually have been made, and in reality the number is often above 100 percent. Meeting the needs of disgruntled customers is a difficult job. In addition, employees frequently move from one company to another to get a bit more pay in the booming Indian economy or end up trying other starter jobs in telecom or retail.

I don't remember exactly what I said to Malhotra, but it was roughly "I don't know, but I'll bet I can come up with something that would interest both of us." I spent my free time during the rest of the trip, along with the twenty-hour journey back to the United States, considering his question. Until then, most of my research had concerned learning by doing. But if a large percentage of workers might leave in the first few months, interventions that took a long time to roll out would be doomed from the start. When I returned home, I started bouncing ideas off my frequent collaborator Francesca Gino. She and I recognized that we needed to talk to someone who had spent more time looking at individuals' onboarding experiences. Fortunately for us, Dan Cable, our UNC colleague at the time, did just that type of work. We began discussing ideas, and partway in we realized that we were being too incremental. We needed to ask a different question: What change would reduce attrition, but the company will never say yes? We figured that such an approach would produce some outlandish ideas that we could then pare back to get company approval. Quickly our discussion coalesced around one individual-focused intervention. We loved it so much that we pitched it to Wipro's leaders, and to our great surprise and delight, they said yes. They agreed to give us one hour of each onboarding employee's time on the first day to run an intervention. This is what we put together:

Our primary focus was on releasing each person's individuality. We thought a relatively small nudge might have a big effect. So we tried to make the hour all about the individual. In the first fifteen minutes he or she heard from a senior leader at the company who talked about how working at Wipro enabled people to be themselves and identify their own opportunities. The employee then spent fifteen minutes on a problem-solving exercise before being asked to reflect for fifteen minutes about how he or she could be an individual at work. Then the employee used this identity to introduce himself or herself to the others in the room. When these new employees left, we gave each of them two fleece sweatshirts and a badge with their names on all three.

Originally, we thought we'd simply compare this treatment group with a control group that had received no intervention. But we realized that people might just like free stuff, so we created an organization-focused condition: The senior leader spent fifteen minutes discussing Wipro's values and what makes the company outstanding. (These jobs were highly sought after, and only a small number of workers were selected.) A star performer then discussed the same things, and people had fifteen minutes to reflect on what made them proud about working for Wipro. During the final fifteen minutes, they discussed their answers as a group. Then the workers were sent on their way with sweat-shirts and badges bearing the company name rather than their own.[19]

That was it. We changed one hour on the first day, and then everyone went through the same training for fourteen weeks before heading out to the production floor to begin working. The job itself didn't change—only the framework for being oneself. We believed in our heads and hearts that the intervention would have a positive effect, but we couldn't know for sure until the data came in, months later.

That summer, we gathered as a research team in my office in the McColl Building on UNC's campus to learn what had happened. Often the analyses we do require arduous hours to set up. But as a first pass, we wanted to give attrition an "eyeball test"—could we see the difference just by looking at the summary statistics? I worked to prepare the data as Gino and Cable watched on my monitor. Finally it was ready, and we all leaned forward when I hit "Enter."

I recall silence when the table first appeared on the screen. Slowly large grins broke out across our faces as we realized we were seeing a huge effect. Attrition among employees in the individual treatment was more than 20 percent lower than attrition among employees in either the organizational treatment or the control group. Subsequent analyses with sophisticated regression models revealed the same pattern and also produced evidence that in some cases customers, too, were more satisfied.

As a follow-up, we conducted lab experiments with stu-dents in which we tried to mimic the Wipro setting. We had similar interventions, and students then did data entry. We invited them back the next day as a proxy for attrition (if they didn't come back, we counted them as "leaving the organization"). We again found an overwhelming impact from the individual treatment. Additional analyses revealed the driver of our effect: workers given the individual treatment reported higher levels of authentic self-expression, which led to less turnover and better performance in their work.

Releasing the individual is powerful and potentially quite straightforward. Take time to think about how you can be yourself at work and then do it. As Andrew says in the movie *The Breakfast Club*, "I mean we're all pretty bizarre! Some of us are just better at hiding it, that's all."[20] Think about how you could be a bit more bizarre to learn. If you're a leader, encourage those around you to do it. By reflecting on what you find meaning in, you can be more yourself and learn more. Release the individual!

Well, let me qualify that a bit. Although we do want to bring our authentic selves to work, it's worth remembering balance. We need to be respectful of others and of the rules and norms of the organization; our aim should be *optimal distinctiveness*.[21] Differences enable us by motivating us and leading us to pursue broader ways of learning, but they can also lead others to accord us status. For example, when a professor shows up in class wearing a suit with red shoes, or a luxury shopper arrives in a store wearing sweatpants, observers assume that they must be of high status or they wouldn't behave so distinctively.[22]

Optimal distinctiveness theory points out that if we take it too far—completely flouting the norms of those with whom we need to interact—our differences become a problem. Research by Alison Wood Brooks, Bradford Bitterly, and

Maurice Schweitzer on telling jokes illustrates the point.[23] The researchers found that when people told successful, appropriate jokes, they were judged to be competent and of high status. But people who told unsuccessful, inappropriate jokes were judged to be incompetent and of low status.

The challenge is to be authentic but not outlandish. The advice holds: you must release the individual if you want to learn. But as with many things, moderation is important. Overdoing it, as defined by the situation you're in, will create problems for you and others. This balance applies directly to the teaching I do.

When I first entered the classroom, I again felt like an impostor. I was at the front of the room and looked to as an expert, but did I really know enough? To offset my fear, I tried to take on the personas of the best teachers from whom I had learned—people including Dave Upton, Frances Frei, and Jan Rivkin. But I felt even more fake when I did that, and I could see the skepticism on my students' faces. As I began to be comfortable, I recognized that the only way to succeed was to bring myself into the classroom. And so, over time, my mix of humor (mostly the dorky-dad type), knowledge of the topics, and at times frenetic energy have made for a generally winning combination.

As I settled in even more, I learned the hard way that letting all boundaries go—telling too many stories that struck me as highly interesting but others as tangential, and pacing across the classroom all the while—was a little *too* "authentic." So I've dialed it back a tad, to be myself but not over the top. Occasionally that means telling a joke only in my head (which may be why students sometimes see a random smile when I'm teaching). But the balance permits both me and my students to learn optimally.

As you think about being yourself to learn, design your environment for learning. Wherever you work, find a way to bring yourself into your space. Add a splash of color (artwork, professional or a child's) and photos—for example, a picture of someone you love—or personal mementos, such as a pin commemorating your favorite sports team's winning a championship. If you come to my office, you'll find pictures of my family and friends covering the walls, along with several pieces of artwork—from superheroes painted by my kids when they were young to a professional print of a longhorn steer (I am a proud graduate of the University of Texas, after all). Souvenirs from trips and cities in which I've lived are also on display. All these things make me smile, put me at ease, and create talking points with others when they visit my office.

Finally, I have a small plush Mickey Mouse dressed as the Sorcerer's Apprentice. Years ago, I saw one in a favorite colleague's office and asked her about it. She told me that it helped her when she got stuck. I got myself one, because I knew that seeing Mickey would make me smile. Even better, when I'm struggling and I see Mickey, I think of my friend and what she might do in the situation. (Odds are it would be different from my natural instinct, and most likely successful.) When another friend told me that she was stuck on something, I sent her a Mickey too; now seeing him makes me think of her and how Mickey's magic and my friends' inspiration can help me figure out any challenge.

I came to understand the value of this design slowly. I gradually added things that made me happy and found that I learned more and more effectively in my office. I now know that space and emotions are fundamental to how we learn. So regardless of the amount of space you have, think about how you can put things together that will bring you joy.

A third way to be yourself in order to learn is to identify ways of increasing the ratio of positive to negative feelings in your daily activities. That will help you shift out of the constricting vice that negativity too often creates. As Colin Powell has said, "Perpetual optimism is a force multiplier." The exact ratio isn't scientifically established, but for the vast majority of people, raising it would lead to better outcomes. Shifting your ratio is especially valuable when you have an important learning objective. Before you get started, increase the number of your positive experiences.

There are numerous ways to do this. Think about things you enjoy and try to incorporate them in your work and surroundings. Consider ways to inspire yourself. Research on happiness finds, for example, that doing things for someone else will give you more joy and satisfaction than doing things for yourself. People who were assigned to spend money on a gift for someone else were happier than people assigned to spend it on a gift for themselves.[24] Generating positive experiences doesn't have to involve spending money, of course. You can express gratitude to someone who has helped you learn. Write a letter to a former teacher or mentor, or better yet, pick up the phone and call.

We think we need to fit in to our surroundings to succeed. But the opposite is true—at least up to a point. Others don't look down on us when we allow our individuality to show. When we're authentic, they respect it, and it positions us better to learn. Bob Sutton quotes Warren Bennis, the late, great management thinker who described the stifling nature of trying to be like everyone else: "The best you can be is a perfect imitation of those who came before you."[25] Don't fall prey to that fate. Instead, be yourself. You'll be more positive, more motivated, and able to engage in more open learning.

Chapter 7

PLAYING TO STRENGTHS, NOT FIXATING ON WEAKNESSES

My powers are ordinary. Only my application brings me success.

—Isaac Newton

In early 2002 I was at a crossroads. In June I would graduate with an MBA from Harvard Business School, so it was time to pick a job. After what I considered to be a great deal of thought and careful investigation, I had decided to focus on opportunities in consulting and private equity. I eventually faced a choice between fantastic options in each industry—McKinsey & Company in consulting and a well-regarded venture capital firm that focused primarily on technology and health care services growth companies. I made lists, talked to friends and mentors, and spent a lot of time in prayerful consideration with my wife.

Numerous factors were relevant to the decision, but after all my analysis, two stood out. McKinsey would further hone my skills in analysis and collaboration. I loved both activities and believed that I was at my strongest when I was working with other smart, talented people to analyze complex problems.

The venture capital firm would push me in a very different direction—most likely that of an entrepreneur. I wanted to create things, and I had watched my uncle and parents successfully start and run an enterprise software company. Plus my brother was about to sell his own successful startup. I knew that if I wanted to succeed as an entrepreneur, I would have to improve my ability to sell. The VC job had numerous attractive aspects, but a key element was that the firm had a sales-focused model, and I would be spending three out of every four weeks traveling to various cities to identify new deals and sell us as partners. When I was in the office, a good portion of my time would be occupied with cold-calling prospects.

I saw my lack of ability at sales as a weakness that would prevent me from achieving my long-term objectives. I decided that joining the VC firm would address that weakness, whereas McKinsey would deepen my existing strengths. Off I went to join the venture capitalists.

During my time at the firm, the people were interesting, the work was engaging, and I dutifully cold-called and worked on my sales skills. Although I wasn't eager to sell, when pushed into an environment where it was required, I could do it—and I got better. But the fit was weak. I didn't love what I was doing, and in all honesty, my performance was only adequate. I put in the time and I tried hard, so I wasn't the worst venture capitalist ever, but I wasn't close to the best. Chastened,

I stepped back, reconsidered where my strengths were, and ended up on a path toward business academia.

With the benefit of many years of studying learning, I now appreciate that I made an all-too-common mistake. Instead of finding ways to leverage my strengths, I fixated on my weaknesses. The advice I would now give my younger self is don't try to fix irrelevant shortcomings. We learn best when we play to our strengths—those capabilities at which we excel. They are motivating. A primary driver of motivation is the ability to master a task.[1] We can force ourselves to learn things that are distasteful to us, just as we can force ourselves to eat lousy-tasting vegetables that are good for us, but as any parent will tell you, if you make the vegetables appetizing, healthful eating is suddenly not so hard after all. The same is true of learning. Working on tasks for which you have a natural aptitude provides both internal and external benefits.

Our progress often returns us to a childlike state of wonder as we discover new things. Albert Einstein said, "That is the way to learn the most, that when you are doing something with such enjoyment that you don't notice that the time passes. I am sometimes so wrapped up in my work that I forget about the noon meal."[2] Think about your own life—when was the last time you got so caught up in your activities that you forgot about a meal? Like making new discoveries, the little subtasks that we complete along the way to larger goals keep us engaged and motivated.[3] When we focus on our strengths, those positive effects are more likely.

As well as creating motivation, strengths can change other internal states—including health. Research shows that when people use their strengths during the day, they are likely to report feeling energetic and well rested.[4] To understand this in more detail, Julia Lee, Dan Cable, Francesca Gino, and I conducted our own study.[5] We randomly assigned subjects to two groups: one would engage in what's called the Reflected Best Self Exercise (more about this later), and the other would not. In the research laboratory we collected a saliva sample from each subject to identify levels of secretory immunoglobulin A, an antibody that helps the body defend against colds and other infections by limiting the ability of bacteria and viruses to adhere to mucosal surfaces. Then the members of the treatment group read reports about their strengths, and those in the control group wrote about their daily routines. Roughly thirty minutes later we collected saliva samples again. Subsequent analysis revealed that subjects who had done the strengths exercise did in fact see a strengthening of their immune systems.

Strengths can create external motivation as well, because achieving goals leads to praise and recognition from others—a key driver of performance. We seek such recognition, and we'll actually pay for it. For example, UCLA professor Ian Larkin studied sales professionals at a large enterprise software company where those who finished in the top 10 percent were rewarded with membership in the Sales Club.[6] That included an email of recognition to the entire company from the CEO, a vacation in Bermuda with the other club members, and a gold star on one's card. Such recognition has value, but how much? In his analysis, Larkin found no long-term performance difference between people who just made it into the club and those who just missed. When he asked the sales professionals how much they would pay to be a member of the club, they reported an average of $1,000. Given the associated prestige and recognition, it's not surprising that people valued membership.

The context provided a way for Larkin to estimate the club's actual value, not just what people said it was. The company's compensation plan was complicated, and about 20 percent of the sales professionals would make more money if they waited until the first quarter to book a commission as opposed to doing so in the fourth quarter. However, booking it in the fourth quarter would increase the likelihood of getting into the club. After careful modeling, Larkin found that on average, by booking their sales sooner rather than later, the salespeople ended up paying $30,000 (5 percent of their pay) to join the club. That's how powerful recognition from others can be.

The same principle applies to thinking about strengths and learning. When you use your strengths, you're not only engaged but also more likely to succeed. Others notice and give you feedback, creating a virtuous cycle. You want the validation to continue, so you look to improve and use your strengths.

Here's another example of how strengths can be both internally and externally motivating. Evidence and experience suggest that most people are not engaged at work. For many years the Gallup Organization has surveyed work engagement globally. The response is perhaps not shocking, but it is disheartening: in 2016 only 33 percent of US workers and 13 percent of global workers reported that they were engaged on the job.[7] Gallup asks a number of other questions in the survey and has consistently found that the answer to whether or not one regularly uses one's strengths at work is the most predictive of work engagement. People who use their strengths are six times as likely as those who do not to report that they're engaged.[8]

Challenges in Learning from Strengths

If strengths are such a powerful tool for learning, why don't we use them more often? Because we focus on fixing our weaknesses while struggling to identify our strengths.

It seems counterintuitive in a book about learning to argue that we should ignore our weaknesses. Weaknesses practically define what we choose to learn. Think about how performance reviews work in most organizations. Whether the data is collected from inclusive 360-degree reviews or from a manager alone, comments are provided as a "feedback sandwich." A few perfunctory, positive comments are provided at the beginning and the end—the bread—and the bulk of the time is spent focusing on the things that need attention—the employee's weaknesses—that make up the meat of the conversation.

We tend to dwell on the things that go wrong and want to fix them. But that's because we believe that we need to excel on all dimensions to achieve long-term success. After business school, I believed that I would have to identify any and all weaknesses and eliminate them to accomplish my objectives. If I could simultaneously be a great strategic thinker, carefully analyze all situations, empathetically interact with others on my team, compellingly share my vision internally and externally, and eventually sell my idea, I would be successful. And it's true: if I had been able to do all those things at a high level, I certainly would have improved my chances of success. But unfortunately, like most people, I have strengths in some areas and weaknesses in others. Moreover, there are only twenty-four hours in a day, so if I choose to spend time addressing my weaknesses, I forgo the opportunity to further develop my strengths. Finally, in many cases weaknesses are things that one is not only not good at but also unlikely to become good at. Even with attention, they may not improve much.

The same lessons can be true for organizations. Many organizations have no clear idea of how their policies and decisions come together to form a logical set of capabilities. These choices make up an organization's operations strategy. A good operations strategy is one in which the organization does things in a way your customers value more than your competitors' approach so that the organization can create and capture value. Examples abound of companies' attempts to be all things to all people—the lowest-cost, highest-quality, most innovative, ecofriendly, good-health solution in the marketplace! My friend Tom Fishburne's cartoon, below, captures the idea beautifully.[9]

© marketoonist.com

Instead of trying to be everything to everyone, decide what you'll focus on and what you'll say no to. Zara, the largest brand of the world's largest retailer, Inditex, is a wonderful case in point. Zara helped invent the concept of fast fashion, in which the retailer observes what fashions are trending and quickly gets them into stores—a more complicated proposition than it sounds, given that the industry traditionally operated with long lead times for design, sales, and manufacturing. With more than two thousand stores in almost ninety countries, Zara has been wildly successful, and others have sought to imitate it. Zara's operating model includes numerous innovations, from empowered store managers who help set their stores' collections to active commercial personnel who look for trends to fast design and deployment of those trends. But two of its choices deserve special attention.

First, the brand decided to vertically integrate its operations: it designed and manufactured its own products and sold them in its own stores. It outsourced some steps, such as sewing, but Zara's level of involvement throughout the supply chain was significantly greater than that of competitors, which typically outsource manufacturing and sometimes even parts of product design.

The second choice was even more counterintuitive. Zara chose to locate much of its manufacturing in high-cost areas in Spain and elsewhere in Europe. At a time when competitors were rushing to Hong Kong, China, Bangladesh, and Vietnam, Zara swam against the tide. It realized that to be fast—which is what its customers valued—it would have to accept certain weaknesses, such as a higher-cost manufacturing position.

A traditional weakness framing would have eliminated Zara's very advantage. Yes, its manufacturing costs may be higher, but by focusing on its strengths—getting the right product to market as fast as possible—it learned, improved, and succeeded in the marketplace. Once a fashion becomes a hit in the retail marketplace, retailers want to offer more of it; but if the manufacturing and delivery cycle takes six to nine months (or more), that isn't feasible. Zara's model solved that problem and made it harder for others to copy its strategy.

Zara's clothes are not designed to last for many years; the company competes on speed and fashion, not on quality and durability. For me, that's a disqualifier. I have a suit from my senior year in college that I still wear, and my dress shirts don't get retired until my wife points out that the collars are fraying. (Even then, she sometimes has to throw them away surreptitiously.) But Zara knows that I—a university professor who still wears a twenty-year-old suit—am not its target customer. That customer wants to wear a garment a few times and then move on to something new. If Zara were to address the "weakness" of clothing longevity, it would just add cost with no clear advantage; the clothes still wouldn't appeal to me or add value for its core customers. Zara recognizes the need to say no to many possible choices. It focuses on the operational aspects that allow it to excel at serving its customers—its "order winners."[10] (Based on professor Terry Hill's order winner theory, an order winner is the performance outcome that leads a customer to choose a product or service.)

You can use this same logic in thinking about your learning goals. Say no to the idea that any weakness must be treated as a learning need. Instead, focus on the key qualities that enable you to create value and differentiate yourself. Your strengths can become your order winners.

The other challenge is identifying our strengths. We often struggle to assess ourselves accurately. The failure to do so is sometimes called the Lake Wobegon effect, in reference to the fictional town of Garrison Keillor's *Prairie Home Companion*, "where all the women are strong, all the men are good looking, and all the children are above average."

When teaching decision making, I drive this point home with a simple exercise. I take a poll by asking participants, "Relative to others in the class, what percentile would you rank your _____," filling in the blank with qualities from driving to academic performance to the ability to deliver results. Because the question asks for a relative rank, an accurate assessment across the entire group would average out at the fiftieth percentile. Nevertheless, individuals consistently rank themselves as above average.

A survey of one million high school seniors revealed that 70 percent believed they had above-average leadership skills.[11] Other studies are consistently similar. For example, a series of experiments explored why people incorrectly assume that they are more generous and kind than others.[12] Two possible explanations exist. One is that they may be too skeptical about the generosity of their peers—maybe people are nicer than we think. The other is that perhaps they're accurate about others but wrong about themselves. Consistently the researchers found that the latter explanation was correct—we think we are more selfless than we actually are.

There are numerous other examples of the same effect.[13] Business leaders report that their companies are more likely to succeed than others in the industry. Intelligence analysts, medical professionals, and psychologists all overestimate the accuracy of their work. My profession is not immune: 94 percent of professors say that their work is above average. In a study within one company, researchers found that on average, individuals rated their own performance in the seventy-eighth percentile, and only 2 percent of participants rated themselves below the fiftieth percentile.[14]

Such misleading views of ourselves suggest that we do indeed struggle to identify our strengths. Unless you are unusually insightful (and if you're nodding and saying "That's me," then reread the two previous paragraphs; some of us are wrong, but I don't know which ones), you are going to incorrectly assess yourself.

Fortunately, we can turn to others for assistance. It turns out we're good at assessing others' strengths. Julia Lee, Dan Cable, Francesca Gino. and I studied this, both in the field and in the laboratory.[15] We worked with a global consulting company, which hires thousands of workers worldwide each year, in its onboarding operations. We wanted to understand how strengths identification might change the way people worked with the company, so we randomly assigned almost 1,400 workers to one of three conditions: The first condition was our control—people went through the normal two-day onboarding process. In the second, we used an hour to encourage people to identify their own strengths. They watched a short video on strengths, discussed the concept with a trained facilitator, and then reflected on their individual strengths. In the third condition, people reflected but also reached out to their social networks to get them to provide feedback to the researchers. They were told that they were being given "the opportunity to gain additional insight into your strengths by reaching out to those who know you best." After the feedback had been gathered by us, it was shared with the individuals in a report.

We then tracked all the participants for the next year. We found that the control group and the group that simply reflected on strengths were indistinguishable on numerous measures of how they viewed the company and their own performance. But the group that received strengths information from outsiders had a statistically significant different reaction. These people were less likely to report burnout in their jobs, less likely to report a desire to leave their jobs, and more likely to report a strong relationship with the company. Input from outsiders helps us more accurately identify our strengths and then benefit from them at work.

We repeated our analyses in a controlled laboratory environment using three similar conditions: a control, a treatment where participants identified their own strengths, and a treatment where participants got feedback from outside partners. After the strengths exercise, we asked them to prepare a three-minute explanation of why they should be hired for their dream job. Two raters judged the quality of the presentations. As with our field study at the consulting firm, we found that those who received feedback were statistically more likely to outperform the other two groups.

Successfully Learning from Strengths

To learn from your strengths, you must first identify them. Doing this alone is challenging. But others can give you powerful insight into your own abilities. Fortunately, a tool can aid this process—the Reflected Best Self Exercise (RBSE). Originally developed by researchers at the University of Michigan, the RBSE is seemingly simple.[16] You identify ten to fifteen people who know you well. Part of the power comes from a diversity of feedback providers, so think broadly. Yes, you may include a manager or a coworker, but also include former colleagues, old friends, your college roommate, family members, a professor who mentored you, and others you think have unique insights into who you are when you're at your best. Take time to identify your ideal choices—as with most things, the more up-front work you do, the more benefit you'll see later on. The Center for Positive Organizations at Michigan, or a company such as Essentic, can run the process for you.[17] Alternatively, you can do it yourself by reaching out to your feedback providers and asking them to identify two to three times when they saw you at your best and accomplishing things that were meaningful to them.

One advantage of having an outsider conduct the process for you is that it can consolidate the stories and weed out any that don't meet the goal. (Sometimes feedback providers struggle to follow instructions and revert to sharing opportunities for improvement.) If you do it yourself, ask a friend to compile the stories for you—maybe you can do the same in return. Once the full report is ready, carve out a block of time and find a place to be alone. Reading these reports can be an emotional experience. You hear about the positive impact you've had on the people who know you best.

Some stories may be old family favorites. Were I to write one for my mother, I would discuss her tenacity and illustrate it with the story of when she took me as a child from Austin to San Antonio for a swim meet. The rest of the team canceled because of icy roads, but we just went very slowly— all because she knew I desperately wanted to qualify for the state championships. When I failed to qualify, she showed her compassion by encouraging me to take the one last available opportunity (which I did, with success).

Some of the stories may be about things you've forgotten or things you didn't realize had made such an impact on those around you. For example, were I to write a story for my wife, I would discuss her ability to be welcoming and inclusive. As a college student, she was a teaching assistant for a country-dance class. I remember watching her fly around the room—making everyone feel like a good dancer who with a little more work could become an excellent one. I doubted that her perspective was accurate with regard to me, but she so thoroughly believed in me (as she does in everyone she meets) that I knew failing would be letting her down, and I could not do that.

After reading the stories, and perhaps shedding a few tears, try to identify themes and strengths. Think carefully about what underlying capabilities stretch across these stories—in particular, those that highlight your unique value and that you also enjoy using. Then reflect about how you can use them more often at work.

Creating an action plan is also important. Reflecting on your strengths may make you feel good, but don't let that be a flash in the pan. If you make a plan to use your strengths more often—at work, at home, in your volunteer organizations—they are likely to stick. Recognize that you often have some control in all those domains. For example, researchers partnered with Google to examine the impact of identifying strengths and then creating action plans (through what's called the Job Crafting Exercise); they found that people who went through the planning exercise were rated by peers as happier and more effective in their jobs six weeks later.[18] If you don't see a way to use your strengths more at work, consider skills-based volunteering or other means of deploying them. Your learning should increase, and that will spill over to multiple facets of your life.

The second step in learning from strengths is to take a careful look at your weaknesses. Another part of Terry Hill's order winner theory applies here as well—order qualifiers, which are necessary but not sufficient to secure a sale.[19] They are the ante to get into the card game. If you don't have the ante, you'll just have to watch, but even after you put it in, more must be done to take home the pot.

How do order qualifiers help us understand weaknesses? True, we can't be good at everything, but that doesn't mean we can ignore all our weaknesses. Which ones should get your attention? Those that serve as your order qualifiers. Call these your critical weaknesses. During my time at the venture capital firm, I came to appreciate that it was not the right long-term job for me, but it had helped me gain clarity on what my strengths were. Through my work and through many conversations with my wife, my brother, and close friends and mentors, I came to appreciate that I had strengths in curiosity, seeing connections between disparate factors, analytical problem solving, and working in groups of talented individuals. As I thought about how to apply those strengths, I realized that business academia might provide an excellent opportunity.[20] Applying to and attending a doctoral program was not just about further developing my strengths. It was also necessary for identifying the order qualifiers that were critical weaknesses standing in the way of my accomplishing the larger goal. For example, I knew very little about how to analyze a large data set to find patterns (econometric analysis). It's still not what I would call a strength, I do not create new methods for other researchers to use, but I worked with great faculty members like Rob Huckman and took enough econometrics courses to ensure that I could do the econometrics necessary to leverage my strengths for learning and differentiation.

Think about the weaknesses that can help support your strengths and go after those.

Finally, a note of caution. We need to recognize that over-confidence can turn strengths into weaknesses. The Swiss German philosopher Paracelsus, generally regarded as the founder of toxicology, wrote, "All substances are poisons; there is none which is not a poison. The right dose differentiates a poison from a remedy."[21] This is sometimes distilled down to "The dose makes the poison," an extraordinarily important insight.[22] Too much of a good thing is still too much. (You can readily observe this if you put a Staats man in front of a tub of Blue Bell ice cream.) We have to be careful not to become so blinded by our strengths that we lose control—either growing arrogant or ignoring important signs around us.

For example, in a study Diwas KC, Francesca Gino, and I looked at how negative news from the FDA about drug-eluting stents affected cardiologists' subsequent choice of stents for their patients.[23] We found that doctors who had more experience using drug-eluting stents were more likely to ignore the FDA advisory. Since we couldn't conclusively determine whether this choice was appropriate (the data suggested it was not), we ran multiple laboratory studies to show that when individuals had more expertise, they were more likely to continue on an unproductive course.

I now realize that I was never going to excel at generic selling of the cold-calling variety. I could do a passable job, but it wasn't a strength or a passion. I did learn, though, that I was quite good at and enjoyed relationship selling—really getting to know someone and learning how we might work together. Given time, I could understand another's perspective and come up with creative ways to address his or her needs as well as my own. That strength has been a key success factor for me as I partner with academic colleagues and with companies on research and consulting projects. I hope you can find your own strengths a little more quickly than I did. Regardless of whether your search is fast or slow—by focusing on your strengths, addressing critical weaknesses, and making sure you use your strengths productively rather than in harmful ways—you'll improve your ability to learn.

Chapter 8

SPECIALIZATION AND VARIETY

Learning is more than the acquisition of
the ability to think; it is the acquisition
of many specialized abilities for
thinking about a variety of things.

—**Lev S. Vygotsky**[1]

In 2003 the noted filmmaker Errol Morris released the documentary *The Fog of War*, a series of interviews with Robert McNamara, the architect of US involvement in Vietnam during the Kennedy and Johnson administrations. The movie intersperses McNamara's reflections on the hard lessons he learned with historical footage, providing a candid look at a man trying to learn from the many difficult situations he faced. My friend Katy Milkman introduced me to the movie, and one scene in particular has stuck with me for many years. McNamara is reflecting on two days during the buildup to the Vietnam War. On the first, August 2, 1964, a US destroyer, the *Maddox*, was attacked in international waters by a North

Vietnamese patrol boat. Investigators recovered evidence in the form of North Vietnamese shells, so it was clear that an attack had occurred. The challenge, though, lay in learning the intent of the North Vietnamese. Was this a sign of escalation or just an isolated incident? President Johnson, with the advice of McNamara, decided not to deploy a military response. But two days later, two destroyers, the *Maddox* again and the *Turner Joy*, reported having been attacked. In McNamara's recounting, this second attack persuaded the United States that the North Vietnamese were committed to all-out war. Johnson, who felt he had no choice but to respond in kind, went to Congress for authorization to take the United States into what became the Vietnam War.

As the experts reviewed the evidence of the attack, it became unclear whether they had actually learned what they thought they had learned. In the documentary, Morris plays recordings from the discussion:

> *Admiral Sharp:* He [Admiral Moore] said many of the reported contacts with torpedoes fired appear doubtful. Freak weather effects on radar and overeager sonar men may have accounted for many reports.

> *9 Minutes Later.*

> *Admiral Sharp:* It does appear now that a lot of these torpedo attacks were from the sonar men, you see. And they get keyed up with a thing like this and everything they hear on the sonar is a torpedo.

> *General Burchinal:* You're pretty sure there was a torpedo attack, though?

> *Admiral Sharp:* Oh, no doubt about that, I think. No doubt about that.[2]

First, Sharp points out that the experts best qualified to assess whether a torpedo has been fired, the sonar men, are likely to get "keyed up" during the most crucial time possible—when an attack occurs—and inaccurately assess the situation. In other words, when they are most needed for their expertise, the experts are most likely to identify a false positive. Second, Admiral Sharp's last line always sparks awkward laughter when I use the video in class. Even though the admiral has just called into question that torpedoes were fired, he responds with certainty that the attack occurred, albeit with a qualifier: "I think." Sharp is the expert in command whose role is to assess the situation and decide how to act, yet he struggles with just that.

The Fog of War continues with Morris and McNamara talking about what happened in those two episodes before Morris summarizes the discussion, saying, "We see what we want to believe."[3]

This is the next key challenge for learning. Expertise is necessary for success and learning, but it's often insufficient. When we become too specialized, we see what we want to believe rather than what is actually there. We think deep specialization is a way to learn, but it may constrain how we understand new material. Learning, therefore, must incorporate variety as well as specialization.

Why Do Specialization and Variety Lead to Learning?

Before considering the value of specialization and variety together, let's think about how they contribute independently to learning. The idea that specializing in a single task leads to improvement has formally existed at least since Adam Smith wrote about it in 1776.[4] That idea grew in importance as the Industrial Revolution spread around the world, creating larger, more complex operations than ever before. Specialization can activate one of the most powerful forces for learning that we know: the learning curve.

Accumulating experience improves performance, even if at a decreasing rate. As we repeat the same task again and again, we get a bit better at it. Learning curves apply to measures other than speed, such as quality, cost, and customer satisfaction, and to teams and organizations as well as to individuals.[5]

We can unpack the concept even further. The noted learning scholar Michael Lapre introduced me to analytical research suggesting that an overall learning curve actually consists of many smaller curves.[6] Combining this with work I was already doing on experience helped me see that task experience is multidimensional. Performing one task, such as a heart surgery or a contact-center call, involves experience with many different things. That call, for example, involves learning about a given product, but also learning about different types of customers, and how to deal with success or failure from a prior call, and on and on. In research I did with Jonathan Clark and Rob Huckman, we found that radiologists learned as they completed procedures, but their understanding deepened when that experience was broken into finer-grained detail—anatomy (a knee, say), technology used (X-ray or MRI), or the customer (one of various hospitals).[7] Each of these involved small learning curves that could be subsumed into the overarching curve.

Variety, too, alters our knowledge and motivates us. When we engage in varied but somewhat related tasks, we bring knowledge from one area to another—a concept referred to as *brokerage*.

The career of Herbert Simon, a professor in computer science, psychology, political science, and administration, provides an excellent example. His groundbreaking ideas helped shape numerous academic fields, from economics to sociology to technology. What gave him such impact was his ability to use ideas from one field to gain fresh perspective on another.

Simon combined his political science and economics training to generate over time a behavioral theory of the firm, eventually demonstrating that we are "boundedly rational"—we use the limited information we have to make the best decisions we can.[8] By recognizing that a core assumption of economics—that individuals are rational, omniscient profit maximizers—was wrong, Simon reshaped the field and was recognized with the 1978 Nobel Prize in Economics.

His use of variety in knowledge across fields persisted throughout Simon's life. As he continued to study human decision making, he realized that computers were a powerful tool for simulating how the process worked. He recognized that they might actually substitute for human decision makers, which led him to a computer science professorship and a foundational role in the field of artificial intelligence.

Like Simon, once you have identified a problem, you can address it in novel ways. You may identify connections that no specialist has seen before if you recognize that part of a solution you used in one context might help you address a challenge in a different setting.[9] Harvard Business School professor Karim Lakhani has studied how "broadcast search"—sharing a difficulty widely—often leads to the discovery of novel solutions from unexpected areas. For example, a protein crystallographer might learn of a toxicology challenge at a pharmaceutical firm and use methods known in her field to generate a solution.[10] Given that most innovations arise from new combinations of old ideas, it shouldn't be surprising that our learning improves when we have a variety of ideas to draw upon.[11]

Variety may prove useful even if it slows you down— perhaps especially when it slows you down. I investigated this idea with my colleagues Rellie Derfler-Rozin and Celia Moore.[12] We were interested in whether what's known as *sequential variety* might lead to more-ethical decision making. Sequential variety describes the order in which tasks are completed. Suppose you need to complete each of the following three tasks three times: A, B, and C. You could complete them together to maximize speed—AAA, BBB, CCC—or interleave them—ABC, ABC, ABC. We hypothesized that although the latter approach might slow you down, it also might engage your slow, conscious, controlled information processing system, rather than your rapid-fire, unconscious, automatic information processing system. The slower approach might lead you to be more thoughtful and not break rules—like those we studied in the field at a bank (such as returning late from a lunch break) or those we created in the lab environment (participants had to push a button to stop the correct answer from appearing on their screen).

Our results strongly supported our hypothesis. Using variety to slow ourselves down makes us more likely to do what we should. This lesson is valuable not only for avoiding rule breaking but also for learning. Variety can switch you out of automatic mode so that you see what is happening around you and make conscious choices to learn.

Variety offers another advantage for learning: it is motivating. Engaging in different activities helps overcome boredom. A focus on learning curves has led managers to identify more-efficient methods and repeat them again and again. This can lead to learning as workers get up to speed, but their learning slows and then stops as they repeatedly execute the same task. Even worse, backsliding can occur if the lessons supposedly learned are ignored. The theoretical benefits of specialization often don't translate into practical benefits. Managers and other knowledge workers must struggle with the cognitive toll from repeating tasks.[13]

One way to overcome this challenge is to vary activities. An assembly-line worker might switch between seat installation and body-part stamping, or a radiologist might move from CT scans to X-rays. When we engage in a variety of activities, we are stimulated rather than disengaged out of boredom. We stay motivated and are more likely to keep learning.

Challenges That Prevent Us from Learning from Specialization and Variety

Whether to take a specialized or a varied approach is a peanut-butter-or-chocolate problem: they're two great tastes that taste great together, as in the old commercial for Reese's Peanut Butter Cups.

Why is neither one sufficient by itself? Specialization is a powerful tool, but doing the same thing over and over again risks boring us. Losing focus can make us miss (or perhaps actively try not to see) improvement opportunities. Furthermore, we limit ourselves when we take a too narrow view of experience. As we specialize in one area, our view that the world works a certain way grows more fixed. For many years, I've had the following quotation on my wall:

> Nothing is more dangerous than an idea,
> when it's the only one you have.
>
> **—Émile Chartier**

A more colloquial way to say the same thing is that when you have a hammer, every problem looks like a nail. We encounter new circumstances, but we fail to learn because we believe that the same old lessons apply. Remember the example from *The Fog of War*: the expert sonar men were trained to hear torpedoes, and by gosh that's what they heard. I frequently see the same challenge in my own field (and also when I look in the mirror). As academics, we have individual areas of expertise, so we deal with every situation using our accustomed approach instead of improving on it or inventing entirely new approaches—learning.

Specialization also may be limiting because when things change, our experience may no longer be applicable. Instead of interpreting the new information as a circumstance that requires an altered worldview, experts may dig in their heels and pull out a hammer—an approach known as *escalation of commitment*: continuing down a path in the face of evidence that one should not.[14] Those who feel more like experts are more likely to escalate their commitment—for example, continuing to invest money in a failed project when they should switch to a better choice.[15] When new and unexpected events occur, experts must confront the possibility that their worldview is incorrect. Variety can help.

Captain Robert Scott's ill-fated attempt to become the first person to set foot on the South Pole illustrates the point. In

1910 Scott set out for the second time to reach the South Pole. His earlier venture, in 1902, had fallen short by only a few hundred miles, and he was determined to make it—especially since Ernest Shackleton had failed in 1909. After eight years spent preparing and exploring, Scott wrote in his journal, "I feel sure we are as near perfection as experience can direct."[16]

Upon reaching the Ross Ice Shelf, his mission launch point, Scott and his team set to work. Bad news arrived swiftly. He learned that the Norwegian explorer Roald Amundsen was also trying to reach the pole and that he'd gotten a large head start. Moreover, Scott had decided to use ponies rather than dogs as pack animals, and the ponies were ill-adapted for the climate. Finally, his team located its main supply depot in the wrong place, dramatically increasing the mission's degree of operational difficulty.

Instead of learning from these challenges and adjusting, Scott chose to press on. He and his five-person team did reach the South Pole, but they arrived five weeks after Amundsen. And on their return journey, the challenges continued to mount. Scott and his men all perished only eleven miles from the next supply depot. As the expression goes, when you're in a hole, stop digging. Experts often fail to do just that.

Yet if we focus too much on variety alone, we won't get deep enough to understand what's really going on. We'll miss important details. Moving across different domains may permit us to see connections, but only if our understanding is deep enough to recognize them.

Variety can also limit the fundamental process of learning. The human brain is a remarkable storage device, but if you don't use your knowledge, you lose it (or at least some of it). You may need to relearn key aspects of an older task when you take it up again after engaging in varied experiences. Diwas KC and I looked at data on cardiothoracic surgeons and the procedures they complete.[17] In one analysis, we found that the surgeons improved their performance, in terms of patient survival, as they completed more procedures. But when more time separated one procedure from the next, performance degraded: they forgot some of their knowledge.

Another learning challenge that comes with variety is multitasking—switching between activities in a short time period. We like to imagine that the human brain works like a computer, executing multiple tasks simultaneously. Unfortunately, that seems not to be true. The brain processes tasks sequentially. When you do two things at once, you're actually working on one and then switching to the other before switching back to the first one.

The proper analogy isn't computers—it's manufacturing changeovers. When making one type of part, a machine operator enters the proper settings so that the machine will produce that part. To make a different one, the operator must reset the machine. This switching cost applies not only to physical changeovers but also to mental ones. In the latter case, the switching cost has three dimensions.[18] First, when you switch to a new task, your brain loads the necessary knowledge into your working memory.[19] Switching among multiple tasks can overload your working memory and impair learning.[20] Second, you need to use your cognitive resources both to load the new task and to inhibit the old one.[21] Third, constant switching can increase stress and impair your performance.[22] All these effects can limit your ability to learn.

Francesca Gino and I studied the impact of constant switching.[23] We examined how learning was affected by changing between tasks for people doing mortgage processing data entry at a Japanese bank. The participants sat at computers with two monitors. On one they saw an application from a prospective borrower; on the other were fields for entering the data. As they completed one task, the next would pop up on their computers. Although changing tasks had no physical cost, we found that the mental cost was significant.[24] As the participants increasingly changed over within a day, improvement decreased. In other words, their ability to learn was constrained.

Successfully Learning from Specialization and Variety

A dedicated learner needs to deploy both specialization and variety, but how? The software company Valve provides a vivid illustration. Valve is an award-winning developer of PC games such as Half-Life, Counter-Strike, Team Fortress, and Portal. In addition, it runs a platform, Steam, which distributes its own and others' PC games. In March 2017 it was estimated that more than 40 million users played games on Steam and that more than 220 million active users were on the platform, generating several billion dollars' worth of revenue.[25]

Gabe Newell cofounded Valve in 1996.[26] He'd spent the prior thirteen years working at Microsoft, serving as a producer on the first three versions of Windows. By the mid-1990s he had sufficient wealth to do anything he liked—which was to start a company with interesting people who enjoyed creating products that would have a positive impact on many people. While working at Microsoft, Newell had learned that Windows was the number-two choice for software on people's PCs. Number one was a game—Doom, a popular first-person shooter—created by a small team in Mesquite, Texas. He believed that software games were the future because they combined technological innovation and entertainment to enable immersive experiences. That insight was the foundation of Valve—a company that would attract the best talent, keep and develop that talent, and stay close to customers. A key element of Newell's approach was that Valve employees weren't told what to do. They had no bosses. People were expected to discover how they could create value and engage in those activities.

Valve's horizontal structure creates immense freedom for workers to engage their creativity and to learn. What kind of people does the company seek to fit this model? Its internal handbook was leaked to the public in 2012, and not long thereafter, Ethan Bernstein, Francesca Gino, and I spent time with Valve hoping to understand its model. The handbook reads, "The most successful people at Valve are both (1) highly skilled at a broad set of things and (2) world-class experts within a more narrow discipline."[27] This describes what is often referred to as a *T-shaped* person. Further on, the handbook reads, "We often have to pass on people who are very strong generalists without expertise, or vice versa. An expert who is too narrow has difficulty collaborating. A generalist who doesn't go deep enough in a single area ends up on the margins, not really contributing as an individual."[28]

Although Valve wants people who are curious and willing and able to move among different areas, if they lack sufficient depth, they may fail to make connections as they shift between areas or miss differences that make a solution correct in one area but a poor fit in another.

How can you become T shaped? Remembering the review of strengths in chapter 7, think about how to tie the depth of your T to things that you both enjoy and excel at. Recognize also that if those two dimensions—enjoyment and excellence—don't match up, you may still be able to engage in the activities you enjoy to increase the width of your T.

We can see how a combination of specialization and variety plays out by returning to the Japanese bank. Switching tasks within a day gradually led to decreased learning, so staying specialized in the short term was valuable. But we found that in the longer term, engaging in a variety of tasks increased learning for the mortgage processors. The advice from that context is clear: stay specialized within the short term, but over time branch out. Think about the T: What are you specializing in and when, and what are you broadening your skills at and when?

To take advantage of specialization and variety, you must understand that success depends on a portfolio of experience. Let's look at the example of Sloan Gibson, another US cabinet secretary, to illustrate the point. Like Robert McNamara, Gibson served in the US military; he graduated from West Point and became an infantry officer with Airborne and Ranger qualifications in the 1970s. After being discharged from the army, he went into the finance industry, where he eventually became the chairman and CFO of AmSouth Bancorporation, a *Fortune* 500 bank. In 2008, following his retirement from AmSouth, he became the president and CEO of the United Service Organizations (USO), which was founded during World War II to support service members and their families. Then, in 2014, Gibson was asked to serve as deputy secretary of veterans affairs (VA) under Secretary Eric Shinseki.

The deputy secretaryship was a stretch position for Gibson. He had deep expertise in leadership, change efforts, customer service, and working with veterans, but none in health care. Reflecting on his experiences, he said, "If there's one thread that ran through my career, I was always given things that were broken to run."[29] He also noted that fixing broken things requires significant learning. You can't continue doing things the same way, nor can you apply a solution exactly as you've seen it done elsewhere; you must learn the intricacies of the situation so that you can craft a new approach to move things forward.

In his first meetings with the senior team at the VA, Gibson saw that his approach to learning about the department's activities was different from others'. His questions clearly dug deeper than the norm as he tried to learn what challenges the organization was facing. He often met with individuals many levels down from him in the organization, an unheard-of practice, to try to learn the messy details that were truth, rather than a sanitized version of what others thought he wanted to hear. From the start he said that his "tolerance for chaos" was perhaps higher than what others in the department were accustomed to. Unfortunately, that tolerance was soon tested.

In February 2014 a program analyst at the Phoenix VA filed a complaint with the federal department's inspector general (IG), saying that personnel in Phoenix, in an effort to hit fourteen-day scheduling targets, were waiting to enter appointments into the system, falsifying records, and sometimes deleting records. In addition to the medical consequences for veterans, who weren't getting needed care in a timely manner, this obfuscation limited the ability to learn and improve. The VA launched a full investigation. The IG found widespread evidence of wrongdoing, and fourteen of the VA's seventeen top leaders, including the secretary, were replaced.[30]

Gibson took over as acting secretary for the department, and President Obama appointed Robert McDonald, a former chairman and CEO of Procter & Gamble, to serve as secretary. McDonald and Gibson were tasked with reforming the VA. During his short time there, Gibson had already learned that the department faced a key challenge. Shinseki "came from a military background," as Robert Snyder, the VA's chief of staff, explained. "He believed in centralized planning, with decentralized execution, and assumed that people would tell him the truth to the best of their knowledge . . . he relied on people to speak candidly, but instead they often told him what *they thought* he wanted to hear . . . [emphasis added]"[31] The former secretary had approached the challenge of running the VA as inherently similar to running the US Army, a job at which he had excelled. Unfortunately, as we've seen, expertise can be blinding. Moving into a new environment requires one to learn and adapt. Gibson's and McDonald's variety of experience had prepared them to learn about and address the numerous difficulties the VA faced.

Gibson and McDonald set out on listening tours to understand the situation. Gibson said, "In the Army I had learned the mantra of 'ride to the sound of the gun.' Throughout my career, when there are problems I've gone right to them to learn and address them. If I don't, who will?"[32] After listening to concerns, both Gibson and McDonald would take immediate action to correct problems that were uncovered. Gibson noted, "Part of what we were doing was modeling good leadership behavior by taking ownership and showing that change was possible." The listening tours were designed for interactions with a diverse group of stakeholders, from people within the VA to veterans and vocal critics. Gibson elaborated, "We were working not only to understand the problems and the many perspectives, but to deliver a powerful message about fixing problems and celebrating the many very positive aspects of VA and specific parts of the operation. This all was designed to be authentic and rebuild trust." As a part of this effort, McDonald and Gibson kicked off a ninety-day plan, "The Road to Veteran's Day," and started with numerous actions, including a performance improvement plan to rebuild trust, improving the delivery of services, and creating a long-term foundation.

The goal of all these efforts was to learn how the organization could provide quality care to veterans while providing value to taxpayers. Gibson's key insight was: "As a health care organization, VA has two massive strategic assets—our scale and our scope. Imagine if we could identify the hundred most important processes that lead to great health care outcomes. What would they be? Imagine that we could identify the best practice inside VA for each and every one of those hundred practices and instill that across the entire enterprise."[33] The senior team focused on building on this insight.

The ensuing two and a half years were a blur of action. McDonald, Gibson, and their team weren't able to complete the transformation of the VA, but it was well on its way by the time they stepped down in 2017, with the change of administration. They had trained more than 150,000 employees in the new approaches and had increased staffing by more than 10 percent to address access and quality issues. Same-day patient access was now available throughout the system; quality measures were high (the VA performed better than the private sector on 96 percent of outpatient measures); and pending claims had been reduced by 90 percent. Moreover, veterans noticed satisfaction scores increased dramatically, even as opportunities for improvement remained.

Capturing the combined benefits of specialization and variety can provide a powerful learning experience. Throughout his time at the VA, and in his prior career, Gibson built his own portfolio of experiences. What types of experience might be relevant in your role? What tasks might you work on? What tools do you need to develop? Who are the customers you serve? Each task is really a bundle of experience profiles. Understanding these different dimensions makes it possible to learn and improve.

Engaging in something new can generate interesting insights.[34] But be careful about just how different things are over time. Research shows that unrelated experience can get in the way of learning.[35] So try to bundle activities that have some underlying relationship. Think about the portfolio of experiences you can build—both now and over your career—to help you learn.

Finally, leveraging specialization and variety together can help you take a novice's perspective—a powerful learning technique. One challenge of gaining expertise is that we forget just how hard things were to learn.[36] Selective memory aids us in some ways—we're willing to try to learn new things that might be hard, rather than just give up—but it also makes us less empathetic toward others who lack our knowledge. When we see things with fresh eyes, we may recognize a challenge that's been staring us in the face all along. As Gibson commented to me, "I think one of the key qualities of a good leader is humility. That is what allows a leader to be open to what he can learn from others."

Combining specialization and variety can be a helpful way to kick yourself back into beginner's mode. First, remember the power of sequential variety. You may sometimes need to slow down to move faster. When you vary the order in which you do things, it can make you pay more attention to each one and find ways to improve. Second, intentionally try to take a novice's perspective, especially in areas in which you have expertise. Also reflect on activities at which you aren't an expert and think about your struggles. Remember what you initially struggled with in your specialized area, and notice what others, be they colleagues, customers, or competitors, struggle with.[37] That may generate novel insights for improvement.

Specialization and variety are both powerful learning tools, but they have potentially serious drawbacks. Instead of treating them as an either-or choice, use them together to help you learn.

Chapter 9

LEARNING FROM OTHERS

I have never met a man so ignorant that
I couldn't learn something from him.

—**Galileo Galilei**

One of my key areas of study as an academic has been how team familiarity—individuals' prior shared work experience—leads to better outcomes. I didn't set out to study this topic, though; I stumbled onto it. In early 2005 I met with my advisor, Dave Upton, who asked me if I wanted to head to Bangalore for a couple of weeks that summer to learn about the application of Toyota Production System principles to software services at Wipro Technologies. I didn't know what I would find, but I knew the correct answer when presented with a chance like that: "Yes!"

The two weeks were a whirlwind. I typically left the hotel at 7:00 a.m. and returned around 9:00 p.m. The days were packed with meetings—with senior executives, project managers, team members, quality managers—one after another.

Our discussions were about their "lean" efforts, but fundamentally we were talking about how individuals and teams learn to deliver results. These meetings planted a number of seeds that would germinate as subsequent research projects—the importance of process, dealing with failure, asking questions, building the right portfolio of expertise, and so on. But at the time, one other idea consistently arose: it wasn't just the repetition of experience with a technology or an industry that mattered; repeated interaction was important. By working with the same team members, individuals found, they learned and dramatically improved their performance.

This idea became the core of my doctoral dissertation at Harvard.[1] I collected data from across Wipro over three years—hundreds of projects, tens of thousands of employees, with countless details on both—for analysis. The finding was as consistent as it was powerful: teams that had worked together before were dramatically more likely to deliver their projects on time, on budget, and with higher quality. Prior experience together was related to a 30 percent decrease in budget deviation and a 19 percent decrease in defects.

Years later, in Project Aristotle (inspired by Aristotle's dictum "The whole is greater than the sum of its parts"), Google found that great team performance, learning, and innovation were less a function of individuals' prior skills than of how the team members interacted and their previous experience with one another.

Talking only about strategies to learn by ourselves overlooks the important role that others play in our learning success. The people with whom we interact are integral to our eventual success or failure.

Why Do Others Lead to Learning?

Others have an impact on your motivation, the process you follow to learn, and the knowledge you acquire. First consider motivation, which has traditionally been seen as one of two kinds—intrinsic (bringing internal rewards) or extrinsic (bringing external rewards).[2] Early research suggested that bad relationships can make us dissatisfied, but they cannot motivate us.[3] For example, a bad relationship with a boss can drive you to leave a job.

But relationships can do more than that. They can improve your health and life expectancy. For example, relationships that generate social support are related to less reported pain and less need for medication.[4] Moreover, connections with others can provide what psychologists now call *prosocial motivation*—a wish to help and encourage others.[5]

Perhaps the most striking example comes from research by Wharton professor Adam Grant and colleagues looking at students working in a fundraising call center for a university.[6] The intervention was simple: some of the participants received a letter from a student expressing gratitude for the fundraisers' work and highlighting how it had enhanced the student's college experience. Those participants not only raised 171 percent more money than the other callers but also spent 142 percent more time on the phone. A tiny connection to the beneficiary drove results and motivation.

Paul Green, Francesca Gino, and I were interested in bringing the relationships even closer—what if we considered coworkers rather than the end user? To do this we worked with an integrated agribusiness company, examining its front-end harvesting operations. We randomly assigned the harvesters to three conditions: (1) external beneficiary—someone outside the company; (2) internal beneficiary—someone within the company; and (3) control group. The first two groups watched a short video of either a customer or a factory employee thanking them for their efforts. We then observed their productivity improvement over time. The data showed that the internal beneficiary group out-performed the external and control groups. A little more research revealed that the improvement was in fact driven by increased motivation from relationships.

Why does military basic training around the world focus on building esprit de corps? Because when we recognize that others depend on us, we are likely to persist in our efforts to learn and improve. Before General Stanley McChrystal took command of the International Security Assistance Force and US Forces Afghanistan, in 2009, he led the Joint Special Operations Command, where he observed the tremendous benefits of keeping units together—not the norm in the US Army's conventional forces. When I talked with him about the lessons he had learned, he said that he had endeavored to keep units together in Afghanistan so that the soldiers could adapt and learn in the new and difficult environment.[7] When we hit roadblocks and aren't sure we can proceed, the relationships around us provide strength and support. This source of motivation is important in the learning journey.

The second learning benefit that comes from others is perhaps the most obvious—they have knowledge that might prove valuable to us. The best illustration I have of this point comes from the smartest person I know—we'll call him James. While we were collaborating in research, I was impressed by how James interacted with new people in many different roles—often people who didn't seem to have much to teach or whose jobs lacked status. I eventually asked, "You have to know you are the smartest person in any room you walk into; how do you still learn?" He told me he recognized that the other person in any conversation knew something (or some things) that he didn't know, and his goal was to figure out what that was and learn it.

When you work with people who have information and experiences different from yours, you have a chance to learn new things. This is one of the oft-cited benefits of fostering diversity in teams.[8] Differences may increase the aggregate knowledge available to individuals. For example, professors Sriram Narayanan, Jay Swaminathan, and Sridhar Balasubramanian found that individual learning among software programmers improved with a more diverse experience set.[9] INSEAD professor Manuel Sosa investigated what factors lead to creativity in dyadic (one-to-one) relationships.[10] He found that individuals at a European software company generated more creative ideas when they had direct ties to others whose knowledge was diverse rather than similar. And Chris Liu, a professor at the University of Toronto's Rotman School of Business, has reached similar conclusions in settings as varied as MIT research laboratories and the US Congress. Liu found that when unexpected circumstances occur—such as a congressperson's desk moving after a colleague loses an election—and lead to an individual's being surrounded by new knowledge, that person is likely to learn and act on that knowledge.[11] Whether you're on a team or working individually, being surrounded by others who have valuable knowledge helps you learn.

We can also better process information when we're surrounded by others. Not only might they share information with us, but we can solve problems jointly. When we interact with others, we can combine our knowledge in new ways and discover novel uses for what we know. We may do a better job of filtering new information, or we may interpret our existing information in different and productive ways.[12] Others may explain something we didn't understand previously or take a different approach that resonates with us.

I've come to appreciate that I do my best work when I interact with others. In isolation I may be able to come up with an interesting way to think about things, but the back-and-forth of having that idea challenged is what tests and thus improves me. In my most frequent and successful collaborations, my colleagues bring significant new ideas, often from different disciplines, along with novel approaches to thinking about and making sense of a situation. Even in the writing of this book, the frequent conversations with and comments from my editor, Tim Sullivan; my wife; and my research collaborators fundamentally shaped what I did. I know that in sharing my explorations with others, I'm sure to hear ideas that will improve my own understanding.

Challenges in Learning from Others

Given the tremendous value in learning from others, why is it such a struggle? First, we tend not to appreciate how collaborative many of our activities are and to discount the important role of others in our own success. The challenge is sufficiently common to have its own name—*coordination neglect*.[13] To study this, Katy Milkman, Craig Fox, and I investigated project teams.[14] These teams were assigned a group task, which you might think would make the others involved far more salient. But even here we saw the struggle.

We focused on individuals' estimates of how long it would take teams to complete various tasks. For example, we showed subjects a human figure constructed from LEGO building blocks and asked them to consider how long it would take a two-person team to build it. Then we asked how long it would take a four-person team. We found that in estimating for the larger team, people tended to focus on the gains that come from the division of labor. They quite reasonably assumed that the task could be divided up and that the multiple team members would take care of their individual pieces of the work. Thus a four-person team might work twice as fast.

But that assumption doesn't account for the necessary coordination. Although each person can do part of the work—say, the right leg, the left leg, the arms, or the head and torso—the figure still needs to be assembled.

We found the same effect when we examined individuals' estimates of the hours required for software projects. The larger the team, the greater the underestimation of the time required. This is consistent with conventional wisdom in industry, which is captured in Fred Brooks's classic *The Mythical Man-Month*.[15] Brooks, the leader of IBM's System/360 computer offering and the founder of UNC Chapel Hill's computer science department, discusses how throwing more person-hours at a software project slows things down considerably, but managers nevertheless see it as a viable solution when they fall behind. This point has been simplified as Brooks's Law, well known to anyone versed in project management: "Adding manpower to a late software project makes it later."[16] We forget all the coordination that is required as we bring in new people.

You can probably discern the challenge for learning. We view work as divisible tasks that can be tackled individually. The same coordination we need to improve efficiency is also necessary for learning. We must recognize and address the myriad interconnections to truly understand the complex work we undertake. Yet we tend to neglect them when we focus inwardly.

The second challenge in incorporating others into our learning process comes in finding and extracting their knowledge. We don't have a searchable index of all the information others have, so it's not surprising that we don't turn to them for new information. We don't know who knows what or how to ask.

This challenge is compounded in the way we interact with others. When we talk to them, we tend to focus on shared as opposed to unique information.[17] How does that look in practice? Imagine that I'm trying to learn about a new client. I know the client has a very strong technical background, so I'm tailoring my pitch around the technological details. A colleague of mine who worked with the client at a previous company knows in addition that he is influenced by a bigger value proposition in making decisions. When we start discussing the client, we are likely to focus on the technical background. We might not even mention the value proposition point.

This occurs for two reasons. First, we tend to look for information that is consistent with our existing views. We begin by asking questions about what we already know, not what we don't know. Second, it feels good to talk about what we both know. When we already know what someone is telling us, we also know that it's credible. But that means we may never get to the unshared information that could actually help us learn more effectively.

The third challenge is an interpersonal one. In theory, when we're surrounded by others with differing knowledge, we're able to draw on that knowledge to solve problems and jointly process the information. However, a long line of research reveals that diversity often has a negative impact on learning and performance.[18] When we're surrounded by people with ideas different from our own, we aren't necessarily open to their perspectives. Instead of thinking of the world as a giant jigsaw puzzle and ourselves as all having different shapes to contribute, we tend to believe that we can already see the entire picture, even when we can't. This egocentric bias runs throughout our interactions with others. As Joachim Krueger, a social psychologist at Brown University, says, "Like a totalitarian government, the ego has been said to shape perception in such a way that it protects a sense of its own good will, its central place in the social world and its control over relevant outcomes."[19]

With our detailed, experience-based view of the world, we assume that others see things as we do. The Stanford psychologist Lee Ross calls this *naïve realism*: "a person's unshakeable conviction that he or she is somehow privy to an invariant, knowable, objective reality—a reality that others will perceive faithfully, provided they are reasonable and rational."[20] But often they don't see things the way we do, not because they are trying to be difficult but because they view the world through their own, different knowledge. When we can funnel these differences into productive conflict around a task, we can generate new and insightful ideas. Too often, though, the conflict becomes personal, which impedes learning.

Successfully Learning from Others

How can you incorporate the perspectives of others to improve how you learn? First you must get to know the people you're working with and value the group as a part of individual learning. Professors Nicholas Epley and Juliana Schroeder highlight beautifully how we are not "social enough for [our] own well-being."[21] They investigated individuals' experiences commuting between home and work. In a number of experiments, people predicted that they would be happier on their commutes if they had time alone. The researchers randomly assigned participants to: (1) interact with others during their commute; (2) not interact with others; or (3) follow their usual approach. The results showed that when people interacted with others, they were happier and at least as productive. Moreover, subsequent studies revealed that people had incorrectly predicted what would happen because they were wrong about how others would view the interaction—it turns out that we often like to have others interact with us.

Reaching out to others even before you need help builds a foundation for future interactions. Asking other people questions makes them feel knowledgeable and leads them to like you even more.[22]

Shifting your mindset to focus on interactions with others is not always easy. I must admit that I have too often viewed them as "wasted" time that wasn't spent "working" on something. That's wrong. Through slow and at times painful introspection, I've come to realize that those interactions are absolutely "working" time. They are an investment in longer-term learning and—in keeping with the research—I find they are typically fun and motivating, because when I'm surrounded by people I care about and with whom I identify, we all work harder and learn more.

The second step is finding ways to work with the same people repeatedly. Just as repeating a task contributes to the learning curve, repeating interactions confers learning benefits. Much of my work has involved studying this in the context of teams, but whatever the setting, such interactions create a foundation for learning.[23]

When I visited with surgeons at UNC's ambulatory care center, where outpatient surgeries occur, a number of them complained about the constant churn of staff members in the operating room. Unfamiliar staffers would not understand the surgeons' cues or comprehend requests, so learning opportunities would be lost. Robert Booth, the orthopedic surgeon described in chapter 3, has built a process for learning that not only evaluates the task but also keeps as much of the staff together as possible. When he moved to a new hospital, he sought to take with him not only his OR staff but also behind-the-scenes people involved in the process, including central supply and housekeeping workers.

Think about the difference in impact on learning in those circumstances. In the first case, a surgeon wastes his time moving equipment back where it should be and grows increasingly frustrated. In the second case, Booth has moved past getting the basic interactions right, and he and his entire team are focused on learning and improving the process.[24]

In my work in software, consulting, and health care, I've observed that repeated interactions create several benefits for learning.[25] First, they help us better coordinate our activities. As we work together, we learn basics, such as a common language. Repeated experience creates structure—both in how we talk and in what we talk about—so that we can move forward.[26] For example, I have come to appreciate the differing ways in which I work with my frequent collaborators. One is a stickler for detail, and with that person I have found that the best strategy is to roll with the choices and edits. If we are to learn and work together fruitfully, I can't worry about small, relatively unimportant details, or we'll never get to the bigger issues. With another, who I know won't look at any small details, I have to, or big troubles may arise later and prevent learning. My coauthors have no doubt figured out strategies for working with me as well. Repeated interactions let us coordinate so that we can allocate attention to the important work around learning.

The second benefit is finding the right knowledge. The late Harvard psychologist Daniel Wegner described the challenge of trying to find out who in a group knows what.[27] He suggested that when we work with others, we develop what he labeled a *transactive memory system* (TMS). A TMS can be used to store knowledge about who knows what and then retrieve it. Working with others gives us an opportunity to develop a TMS, and repeated interactions make it more sophisticated.[28]

The third benefit is that we can respond better to change as we integrate others' knowledge. If the only constant is change, then we must continually adapt. That means quickly finding and using the right knowledge—which typically comes from other people. When we work with the same people, we're more likely to build trust and therefore to use the valuable knowledge we've found.[29] That leads us to take more risks as well. So all together—with a better location of knowledge, transfer of knowledge, and use of knowledge—learning improves.

But does familiarity breed contempt? In the most comprehensive study I've seen on the topic, Northeastern professor Ralph Katz found that research team performance at first improved with repeated interactions but then declined.[30] Over time team members became more inward-focused in their knowledge search—they talked with people on their own teams rather than with people on other teams. Nevertheless, familiarity is rarely problematic. Only when the entire team stayed together for more than five years did performance degrade. How many of us work in unchanging teams for that long? In this day and age, I suspect, not many. I have yet to meet a team that qualifies, despite having interacted with hundreds (thousands?) of teams. So, yes, you should strive not to focus only on those around you as you look to learn, but you're unlikely to reach the limits of repeated interactions.

In general, to improve learning, find ways to work with the same people. The good news is that it needn't be all or nothing. Research shows that even one familiar relationship in a team helps.[31] You probably won't be working with all the same people from one project or task to the next, but just one or two familiar colleagues can help you learn.

You can also improve your learning from others by changing how you interact. One of the challenges of collaboration, as noted earlier, is that we tend to exchange common information rather than unique information, thus limiting our ability to learn. More fundamentally, we often view interactions with others as a competition. For example, when people come together to discuss whom they should hire next or what product feature to include in the product road map, they think about the outcome as either a win or a loss. They take what has been described as an *advocacy perspective*.[32] By advocating their own take on a matter, they try to persuade others that they have the answer, instead of seeking more information about what is really going on. Rather than listening to evidence that might contradict their perspective, they attempt to dismiss anyone who sees things differently. This competitive view severely hampers learning.

Instead of taking an advocacy approach, assume an *inquiry perspective*. Don't try to win the interaction, look to collaborate. Discuss things not to persuade but, rather, to share what you know and critically consider alternatives. When we approach discussions with an openness to different options and a willingness to value people with different perspectives, we are more likely to learn, because we hear others' previously unshared information and we're willing to do something about it.

Here's a helpful analogy: You want a twelve-person jury to decide an individual's guilt or innocence. You have each member of the jury listen to one-twelfth of the trial. Would you then begin deliberations by taking a vote as to guilt or innocence? After hearing only one-twelfth of the trial, would you argue that you could decide the fate of the accused beyond the shadow of a doubt? Of course not. The members of the jury clearly would have very different information. A good foreperson would work to get all the necessary information out on the table.

Typically, though, you have only part of the story, so you need to adopt an inquiry perspective and interact productively with others. To learn, you must gain insight into the eleven-twelfths of the situation that you haven't personally experienced. Remember the approach of the smartest person I know—ask yourself in every interaction what you can learn from the person sitting across the table from you.

Eventually, you need to make decisions in order to move forward, but taking an inquiry approach will make you better able to learn, thus improving the quality of your decisions now and in the future.

The final step in learning from others is reconceptualizing the point of the interaction. Throughout this chapter the focus has been on learning what knowledge others have. But sharing our own knowledge can also benefit us. In the words of Seneca the Younger, "*Docendo discimus*" ("By teaching we are learning").[33] Some people think of teaching as simply imparting knowledge. But it can be a powerful force for learning—and not just for professors. We should all be teachers, regardless of our profession. Teaching others forces us to better understand the topic ourselves. We build confidence in what we're passing along, which can lead to learning, but we also codify the connections we've made to further our understanding. And pupils may raise questions that shift how we approach problems.

I saw the benefits of this while learning the programming language Python with one of my sons. Together we worked on a course online. The experience was rich with learning for me as I listened to the various lessons and then taught him. Because I've written code in many languages, I have the basics down, but there was much Python-specific content to learn. As I taught my son, I found the gaps in my own knowledge, so I knew what I needed to fill. His fresh look at things illuminated new points for me. He also learned by helping his mother understand the basics of Python. It was fun to watch him explaining something to her and, when she asked him a question he couldn't answer, rushing back to figure it out before bringing her the answer and gaining a deeper understanding himself.

With Jonathan Clark and Venkat Kuppuswamy, I explored the idea of learning from teaching within hospitals.[34] We studied hospitals in Maryland and New Jersey, focusing on cardiovascular patients who received percutaneous transluminal coronary angioplasty (PTCA), whereby a surgeon inserts a balloon catheter into a coronary artery and inflates it so that blood can flow around a blockage. We examined more than nine years' worth of data at fifty-two hospitals and found that physicians who taught more intensively learned more from their experience with the procedure, as demonstrated by the fact that their patients were less likely to need further costly procedures. So Ralph Waldo Emerson got it right: "It is one of the beautiful compensations of life, that no man can sincerely help another without helping himself."

We think of individual learning as involving just one person. But that approach is incomplete. Yes, each of us plays a key role in our own learning process, but so do others. We must understand that our learning often depends on others as much as or more than it depends on us. To overcome an inward focus, you need to build relationships, try to repeat your interactions, take an inquiry approach to working together, and teach others. By following that path, you can avoid wasting energy and spend it learning.

Chapter 10

DEE-TERMINATION

The best thing for being sad is to learn
something. That is the only thing that never
fails. You may grow old and trembling in
your anatomies, you may lie awake at night
listening to the disorder of your veins, . . . you
may see the world around you devastated by
evil lunatics, or know your honor trampled
in the sewers of baser minds. There is only
one thing for it then—to learn. Learn why
the world wags and what wags it. That is
the only thing which the mind can never
exhaust, never alienate, never be tortured
by, never fear or distrust, and never dream
of regretting. Learning is the thing for you.

—Merlyn, in *The Once and Future King*

Living in a learning economy means that we must all
approach learning with four mindsets: *focused, fast, frequent,*
and *flexible*. First, you must choose which topics to learn and
then focus on them deeply to gain enough knowledge and
understanding to have an impact. Second, your acceleration
rate matters in learning. You must be able not only to pick the
correct direction but also to get up to speed quickly in that

area. Third, you must always be open to learning: opportunities frequently present themselves, often in unexpected places. Fourth, you must be flexible enough to decelerate and switch to the next opportunity. Focusing on the principles of dynamic learning helps you not only to cope with inevitable change but also to adjust, learn, stay relevant, and excel.

I return to a question that has troubled me since I began this project. If I am such an expert on learning, why do I constantly fail to learn, often making many of the mistakes highlighted throughout this book? That question tumbled around in the back of my mind throughout the writing process (and, frankly, long before that).

The life of an academic is often a solitary affair. I love working with other people, but even joint projects involve long stretches when I'm by myself, doing my part. Writing a book creates even more of those times. The longer I consider the question, the greater my realization that the answer is obvious: learning is hard. If it were not, the work would already be done. Learning is a process that needs constant attention.

I think an apt metaphor is gardening. After I received my MBA, my wife and I moved to Tampa, where we bought our first house. It was a wonderful little home with beautiful flower beds in the front yard. After we moved in, we gave careful attention to those beds, making sure that everything was arranged perfectly and looked beautiful. But then life got busy. We both had demanding new jobs. Being outside in the garden no longer gave us quite the same joy, so we neglected the task. The fact that anything we planted would grow in the rich Florida soil was a godsend for two amateur gardeners, but it also meant that things we didn't want to grow sprouted as well. The beds quickly became overgrown, and the beautiful space was lost. If you looked carefully, you could see the outlines of something special, but otherwise we had little to show for our hard work.

Restoring the garden was arduous—even more work than when we had started out. And that experience maps to learning. Even if you've followed all the principles in this book in the past, you're not finished. You get distracted. Things around you change. Your needs change. Learning is a never-ending process, and if you fail to give it the proper attention, your hard work will be lost.

Learning may be never ending, but you can master the process—provided you have the will. When one of my sons was in preschool, he learned a song in which one line was "I've got determination." When he sang it, he put the emphasis on the first syllable: *dee*-termination. He would simultaneously make a fist with one hand and horizontally punch the other, open hand in front of his chest to punctuate the lyric, scrunching up his face in a determined expression. For the better part of a year, whenever he encountered a difficult task, he would walk around the house singing that he had "*dee*-termination," looking determined, and punching his hand. Now when I am in a deep struggle, I picture him and sometimes punch my own hand.

Yes, learning requires constant vigilance. Yes, when it comes to learning, you can be your own worst enemy. But if you recognize the challenge and seek to overcome it, with determination (and some help from this book), you can. I decided to become an academic to understand how we learn and then teach others about the process. I'd like to believe that my work will help others learn—but I know that it has helped me to do so. Dynamic learners are ready for this process. Happy learning.

Notes

Chapter 1

1. See http://quoteinvestigator.com/2016/12/14/inward/.

2. Bureau of Labor Statistics, "Number of Jobs Held, Labor Market Activity, and Earnings Growth Among the Youngest Baby Boomers: Results from a Longitudinal Survey," August 24, 2017, https://www.bls.gov/news.release/nlsoy.nr0.htm.

3. I. D. Wyatt and D. E. Hecker, "Occupational Changes During the 20th Century," *Monthly Labor Review* 129 (2006): 35–57.

4. G. Will, "A Plan to Make America 1953 Again," *Washington Post*, December 28, 2016.

5. Ibid.

6. S. L. Wang, P. Heisey, D. Schimmelpfennig, and E. Ball, "Agricultural Productivity Growth in the United States: Measurement, Trends, and Drivers," *United States Department of Agriculture Economic Research Report* 189 (July 2015).

7. M. J. Hicks and S. Devaraj, "The Myth and the Reality of Manufacturing in America," Ball State University Center for Business and Economic Research, 2015.

8. M. Dvorkin, "Jobs Involving Routine Tasks Aren't Growing," Federal Reserve Bank of St. Louis, January 4, 2016, https://www.stlouisfed.org/on-the-economy/2016/january/jobs-involving-routine-tasks-arent-growing.

9. A. Smith, *An Inquiry into the Nature and Causes of the Wealth of Nations* (London: W. Strahan and T. Cadell, 1776), 8.

10. American Board of Medical Specialities website, Specialty and Subspecialty Certificates, accessed November 6, 2017, http://www.abms.org/member-boards/specialty-subspecialty-certificates/.

11. B. S. Alper et al., "How Much Effort Is Needed to Keep Up with the Literature Relevant for Primary Care?" *Journal of the Medical Library Association* 92, no. 4 (2004): 429–437.

Chapter 2

1. This section draws on G. Pisano, F. Gino, and B. R. Staats, "Pal's Sudden Service—Scaling an Organizational Model to Drive Growth," Case N9-916-052 (Boston: Harvard Business School, 2016).

2. Ibid.

3. Ibid.

4. E. D. Rothblum, "Fear of Failure," in *Handbook of Social and Evaluation Anxiety*, ed. H. Leitenberg (Boston: Springer, 1990), 497–537.

5. S. Croes, P. Merz, and P. Netter, "Cortisol Reaction in Success and Failure Condition in Endogenous Depressed Patients and Controls," *Psychoneuroendocrinology* 18, no. 1 (1993): 23–35.

6. F. M. Levine, S. M. Krass, and W. J. Padawer, "Failure Hurts: The Effects of Stress Due to Difficult Tasks and Failure Feedback on Pain Report," *Pain* 54, no. 3 (1993): 335–340; and J. H. C. van den Hout et al., "Does Failure Hurt? The Effects of Failure Feedback on Pain Report, Pain Tolerance and Pain Avoidance," *European Journal of Pain* 4, no. 4 (2000): 335–346.

7. E. Kross et al., "Social Rejection Shares Somatosensory Representations with Physical Pain," *Proceedings of the National Academy of Sciences* 108, no. 15 (2011).

8. A. Edmondson, "Psychological Safety and Learning Behavior in Work Teams," *Administrative Science Quarterly* 44, no. 2 (2011): 350–383; A. C. Edmondson, "Learning from Mistakes Is Easier Said Than Done: Group and Organizational Influences on the Detection and Correction of Human Error," *Journal of Applied Behavioral Science* 32, no. 1 (1996): 5–28; A. C. Edmondson, "Strategies for Learning from Failure," *Harvard Business Review* 89, no. 4 (2011): 48–55; and A. C. Edmondson, R. M. Bohmer, and G. P. Pisano, "Disrupted Routines: Team Learning and New Technology Implementation in Hospitals," *Administrative Science Quarterly* 46, no. 4 (2001): 685–716.

9. D. Kahneman and A. Tversky, "Advances in Prospect Theory: Cumulative Representation of Uncertainty," *Journal of Risk and Uncertainty* 5, no. 4 (1992): 297–323.

10. D. T. Gilbert, E. Driver-Linn, and T. D. Wilson, "The Trouble with Vronsky: Impact Bias in the Forecasting of Future Affective States," in *The Wisdom in Feeling: Psychological Processes in Emotional Intelligence*, eds. L. F. Barrett and P. Salovey (New York: Guildford, 2002), 114–143.

11. B. A. Mellers and A. P. McGraw, "Anticipated Emotions as Guides to Choice," *Current Directions in Psychological Science* 10 (2001): 210–214.; D. T. Gilbert et al., "The Trouble with Vronsky"; G. Loewenste in T. O'Donoghue, and M. Rabin, "Projection Bias in Predicting Future Utility," *Quarterly Journal of Economics* 118 (2003): 1209–1248; T. D. Wilson, J. M. Meyers, and D. T. Gilbert, "'How Happy Was I, Anyway?' A Retrospective Impact Bias," *Social Cognition* 21 (2003): 407–432; and D. A. Kermer et al., "Loss Aversion Is an Affective Forecasting Error," *Psychological Science* 17, no. 8 (2003): 649–653.

12. D. A. Kermer et al., "Loss Aversion Applies to Predictions More Than Experience," in T. D. Wilson and D. T. Gilbert, "Affective Forecasting: Knowing What to Want," *Current Directions in Psychological Science* 14, no. 3 (2005): 131–134.

13. R. F. Baumeister, E. Bratslavsky, C. Finkenauer, and K. D. Vohs, "Bad Is Stronger Than Good," *Review of General Psychology* 5, no. 4 (2001): 323–370.

14. Wilson and Gilbert, "Affective Forecasting."

15. B. Weiner, *Achievement Motivation and Attribution Theory* (Morristown, NJ: General Learning Press, 2005); B. Weiner, "A Theory of Motivation for Some Classroom Experiences," *Journal of Educational Psychology* 72 (1979): 676–681; and B. Weiner, *Judgments of Responsibility: A Foundation for a Theory of Social Conduct* (New York: Guildford, 1995).

16. R. P. Feynman and P. D. Sackett, "'Surely You're Joking, Mr. Feynman!' Adventures of a Curious Character," *American Journal of Physics* 53, no. 12 (1985): 1214–1216.

17. The fundamental attribution error is also known as the correspondence bias (L. Ross, "The Intuitive Psychologist and His Shortcomings," *Advances in Experimental Social Psychology* 10 [1977]: 173–220; and D. T. Gilbert and P. S. Malone, "The Correspondence Bias," *Psychological Bulletin* 117, no. 1 [1995]: 21–38.)

18. L. Ross, T. M. Amabile, and J. L. Steinmetz, "Social Roles, Social Control, and Biases in Social-Perception Processes," *Journal of Personality and Social Psychology* 35 (1977): 485–494.

19. D. A. Moore, S. A. Swift, Z. Sharek, and F. Gino, "Correspondence Bias in Performance Evaluation: Why Grade Inflation Works," *Personality and Social Psychology Bulletin* 36, no. 6 (2010): 843–852.

20. F. Heider, *The Psychology of Interpersonal Relations* (New York: Wiley, 1958).

21. D. KC, B. R. Staats, and F. Gino, "Learning from My Successes and Others' Failure: Evidence from Minimally Invasive Cardiac Surgery," *Management Science* 59, no. 11 (2013): 2435–2449.

22. C. G. Myers, B. R. Staats, and F. Gino, "'My Bad!' How Internal Attribution and Ambiguity of Responsibility Affect Learning from Failure," working paper 14–104, Harvard Business School, Boston, 2014.

23. C. Sedikides, "Assessment, Enhancement, and Verification Determinants of the Self-Evaluation Process," *Journal of Personality and Social Psychology* 65 (1993): 317–338; J. I. Krueger, "Return of the Ego— Self-Referent Information as a Filter for Social Prediction: Comment on Karniol (2003)" *Psychological Review* 110, no. 3 (2003): 585–590; and A. H. Jordan and P. G. Audia, "Self-Enhancement and Learning from Performance Feedback," *Academy of Management Review* 37, no. 2 (2012): 211–231.

24. Like many other college students, I matured and began to understand that I'd have to work harder to deal with the increasingly challenging work I encountered. By my junior year I was still performing as I had in my previous schooling, but effort played a much more significant role in my success. Electromagnetics proved a particularly challenging class. My brother was finishing his PhD at the time, and my professor was also on his dissertation committee. After a successful PhD defense, the conversation turned to me, and the professor said, "He is very smart, but he does not apply himself enough." At the time, I took the remark as a compliment; today, with my understanding of the role of effort in learning, I realize it was not.

25. K. D. Elsbach and R. M. Kramer, "Members' Responses to Organizational Identity Threats: Encountering and Countering the Business Week Rankings," *Administrative Science Quarterly* 41, no. 3 (1996): 442–476.

26. P. G. Audia and S. Brion, "Reluctant to Change: Self-enhancing Responses to Diverging Performance Measures," *Organizational Behavior and Human Decision Processes* 102, no. 2 (2007): 255–269.

27. P. Green, F. Gino, and B. R. Staats, "Shopping for Confirmation: How Threatening Feedback Leads People to Reshape Their Social Networks," working paper, Harvard Business School, Boston, 2016.

28. N. J. Roese, "The Functional Basis of Counterfactual Thinking," *Journal of Personality and Social Psychology* 66 (1994): 805–818; L. J. Sanna, S. Meier, and K. J. Turley-Ames, "Mood, Self-Esteem, and Counterfactuals: Externally Attributed Moods Limit Self-Enhancement Strategies," *Social Cognition* 16 (1998): 267–286; I. J. Sanna, E. C. Chang, and S. Meier, "Counterfactual Thinking and Self-Motives," *Personality and Social Psychology Bulletin* 27 (2001): 1023–1034; K. White and D. R. Lehman, "Looking on the Bright Side: Downward Counterfactual Thinking in Response to Negative," *Personal Social Psychology Bulletin* 31, no. 10 (2005): 1413–1424; and P. G. Audia, "Self-Enhancement and Learning from Performance Feedback," *Academy of Management Review* 37, no. 2 (2012): 211–231.

29. X. Lin-Siegler et al., "Even Einstein Struggled: Effects of Learning About Great Scientists' Struggles on High School Students' Motivation to Learn Science," *Journal of Educational Psychology* 108, no. 3 (2016): 314–328.

30. For an organizational example, see the failure report from Engineers Without Borders: http://legacy.ewb.ca/en/whoweare/accountable/failure.html.

31. E. Catmull, *Creativity, Inc.: Overcoming the Unseen Forces That Stand in the Way of True Inspiration* (New York: Random House, 2014).

32. At stickK.com, users can create "commitment contracts," which specify a goal, a timeline, and a cost (such as an amount of money) to help the user accomplish the goal.

33. E. Catmull, "How Pixar Fosters Collective Creativity," *Harvard Business Review* 86, no. 9 (2008): 64–72.

34. R. M. Bohmer, "Fixing Health Care on the Front Lines," *Harvard Business Review* 88, no. 4 (2010): 62–69.

35. This quote is often attributed, apparently incorrectly, to either Abraham Lincoln or Winston Churchill (http://quoteinvestigator.com/2014/06/28/success/).

Chapter 3

1. This section draws on R. M. J. Bohmer, R. S. Huckman, J. Weber, and K. J. Bozic, "Managing Orthopaedics at Rittenhouse Medical Center," Case 9-607-152 (Boston: Harvard Business School Publishing, 2007).

2. R. Booth, "Minimizing Operating Time: Does Speed Kill?" *Orthopedics* 24 (2001): 853–854.

3. Aria—Jefferson Health 3B Orthopaedics website, accessed November 7, 2017, https://www.aria3bortho.org/Physicians.

4. As part of the MIT International Motor Vehicle Program, researchers differentiated between the wasteful processes of American and European auto firms and the "lean" approaches of the Japanese. J. P. Womack, D. T. Jones, and D. Roos, *The Machine That Changed the World* (New York: Rawson Associates, 1990).

5. S. J. Spear, "Fixing Health Care from the Inside, Today," *Harvard Business Review* 83, no. 9 (2005): 78–91; R. M. Bohmer, "Fixing Health Care on the Front Lines," *Harvard Business Review* 88, no. 4 (2010): 62–69; B. R. Staats, D. J. Brunner, and D. M. Upton, "Lean Principles, Learning, and Knowledge Work: Evidence from a Software Services Provider," *Journal of Operations Management* 29, no. 5 (2011): 376–390; and B. R. Staats and D. M. Upton, "Lean Knowledge Work," *Harvard Business Review* 89, no. 10 (2011): 100–110.

6. J. Clear, "This Coach Improved Every Tiny Thing by 1 Percent and Here's What Happened," *James Clear* (blog), http://jamesclear.com/marginal-gains?__vid=c3eef000547a0132ca9c22000b2a88d7.

7. B. O'Keefe, "Leadership Lessons from Alabama Football Coach Nick Saban," *Fortune*, September 7, 2012.

8. Depending on the exact setup, a player will still lose, on average, to the house. By one calculation, she will lose 49.1% of the time, win 42.4% of the time, and draw 8.5% of the time (which occurs when the dealer and the player have the same number, so no money is exchanged). With a model of blackjack, it is then possible to look for opportunities to shift the advantage from the house to the player. For example, if the player can count cards and notices that more low cards than face cards have been played, then the advantage shifts to the player, and she should bet more money. An account of this strategy, loosely based on reality, can be read in B. Mezrich, *Bringing Down the House: The Inside Story of Six MIT Students Who Took Vegas for Millions* (New York: Free Press, 2002).

9. R. E. Bohn, "Noise and Learning in Semiconductor Manufacturing," *Management Science* 41, no. 1 (1995): 31–42.

10. M. Lewis, *Moneyball: The Art of Winning an Unfair Game* (New York: W.W. Norton, 2003).

11. M. Popova, "How Steinbeck Used a Diary as a Tool of Discipline, a Hedge Against Self-Doubt, and a Pacemaker for the Heartbeat of Creative Work," Brain Pickings, https://www.brainpickings.org/2015/03/02/john-steinbeck-working-days/.

12. See https://twitter.com/bcmassey/status/777604654699995136.

13. L. Lefgren, B. Platt, and J. Price, "Sticking with What (Barely) Worked: A Test of Outcome Bias," *Management Science* 61, no. 5 (2015): 1121–1136.

14. Note, however, that close scores during a game may provide additional motivational benefits. For example, J. Berger and D. Pope find that a basketball team that is losing at halftime is much more likely to come back and win the game than is a team that is winning at halftime (J. Berger and D. Pope, "Can Losing Lead to Winning?" *Management Science* 57, no. 5 [2011]: 817–827).

15. To capture factors outside a team's control, the authors look at opponents' made free-throw percentage. Once one has controlled for the number of free-throw attempts, the fact that an opponent made or missed the free throw has nothing to do with a coach's own team. However, even here, coaches were more likely to change strategy after a narrow loss than after a narrow win.

16. R. K. Ratner and K. C. Herbst, "When Good Decisions Have Bad Outcomes: The Impact of Affect on Switching Behavior," *Organizational Behavior and Human Decision Processes* 96, no. 1 (2005): 23–37.

17. Other lab studies show the same pattern in different contexts, such as when evaluating a salesperson's targeting choices (G. W. Marshall and J. C. Mowen, "An Experimental Investigation of the Outcome Bias in Salesperson Performance Evaluations," *Journal of Personal Selling and Sales Management* 13, no. 3 [1993]: 31–47) or a soldier's decision to follow orders (R. Lipshitz, "'Either a Medal or a Corporal': The Effects of Success and Failure on the Evaluation of Decision Making and Decision Makers," *Organizational Behavior and Human Decision Processes* 44, no. 3 [1989]: 380–395).

18. J. S. Lerner and P. E. Tetlock, "Accounting for the Effects of Accountability," *Psychological Bulletin* 125, no. 2 (1999): 255–275.

19. E. S. Elliott and C. S. Dweck, "Goals: An Approach to Motivation and Achievement," *Journal of Personality and Social Psychology* 54, no. 1 (1988): 5–12.

20. S. C. Payne, S. S. Youngcourt, and J. M. Beaubien, "A Meta-Analytic Examination of the Goal Orientation Nomological Net," *Journal of Applied Psychology* 92, no. 1 (2007): 128–150; C. S. Dweck, "Motivational Processes Affecting Learning," *American Psychologist* 41, no. 10 (1986): 1040–1048; C. S. Dweck and E. L. Leggett, "A Social-Cognitive Approach to Motivation and Personality," *Psychological Review* 95, no. 2 (1998): 256–273; E. S. Elliott and C. S. Dweck, "Goals: An Approach to Motivation and Achievement," *Journal of Personality and Social Psychology* 54, no. 1 (1988): 5–12; and C. Dweck, *Mindset: The New Psychology of Success* (New York: Random House, 2006).

21. C. M. Mueller and C. S. Dweck, "Praise for Intelligence Can Undermine Children's Motivation and Performance," *Journal of Personality and Social Psychology* 75, no. 1 (1998): 33–52.

22. C. Dweck, "Talent: How Companies Can Profit from a 'Growth Mindset,'" *Harvard Business Review* 92, no. 11 (2014): 28–29.

23. J. S. Moser et al., "Mind Your Errors: Evidence for a Neural Mechanism Linking Growth Mind-Set to Adaptive Posterror Adjustments," *Psychological Science* 22, no. 12 (2011): 1484–1489.

24. Note that J. A. Mangels et al. similarly find that cognitive activity is higher for those individuals with a learning goal orientation. J. A. Mangels et al., "Why Do Beliefs About Intelligence Influence Learning Success? A Social Cognitive Neuroscience Model," *Social Cognitive and Affective Neuroscience* 1, no. 2 (2006): 75–86.

25. Although it is not germane to our learning discussion, researchers have also explored the relationship between mindset and confidence. Ehrlinger, Mitchum, and Dweck had participants complete a test, but

before giving them their scores they asked the participants to forecast their performance. Participants with a more fixed view of intelligence overestimated their performance by more than 25%, while participants with a more flexible mindset were off by only 5%. The difference was due at least in part to the fact that the fixed-mindset participants had devoted their time and attention to easier problems. Thus one's underlying view of intelligence and learning can have far-reaching implications. J. Ehrlinger, A. L. Mitchum, and C. S. Dweck, "Understanding Overconfidence: Theories of Intelligence, Preferential Attention, and Distorted Self-Assessment," *Journal of Experimental Social Psychology* 63 (2016): 94–100; and H. G. Halvorson, "The Mindset That Leads People to Be Dangerously Overconfident," *Harvard Business Review*, April 19, 2016.

26. B. R. Staats, D. J. Brunner, and D. M. Upton, "Lean Principles, Learning, and Knowledge Work: Evidence from a Software Services Provider," *Journal of Operations Management* 29, no. 5 (2011): 376–390; and B. R. Staats and D. M. Upton, "Lean Knowledge Work," *Harvard Business Review* 89, no. 10 (2011): 100–110.

27. I encourage anyone who is interested in learning to take the time to go back and read Taylor. Over the past century, his writing has been simplified into tropes that sometimes fit what he said and sometimes do not. His work has significant flaws—one sees racism and too often a disregard for workers' contributions—but his underlying thinking about how to improve the craft operations of his time is still relevant today. F. W. Taylor, *The Principles of Scientific Management* (New York: Harper & Brothers, 1911), 109.

28. A. Chen, "The Metrics System: How MLB's Statcast Is Creating Baseball's New Arms Race," *Sports Illustrated*, April 26, 2016.

29. M. Buckingham and A. Goodall, "Reinventing Performance Management," *Harvard Business Review* 93, no. 4 (2015): 40–50.

30. R. E. Silverman, "GE Re-Engineers Performance Reviews, Pay Practices," *Wall Street Journal*, June 8, 2016.

31 Payne, Youngcourt, and Beaubien, "A Meta-Analytic Examination of the Goal Orientation Nomological Net."

32. P. A. Heslin, G. P. Latham, and D. Vandewalle, "The Effect of Implicit Person Theory on Performance Appraisals," *Journal of Applied Psychology* 90, no. 5 (2005): 842–856; and P. A. Heslin, G. P. Latham, and D. Vandewalle, "Keen to Help? Managers Implicit Person Theories and Their Subsequent Employee Coaching," *Personnel Psychology* 59, no. 4 (2006): 871–902.

Chapter 4

1. G. Garrett, "To Lead Is to Acknowledge What You Don't Know," LinkedIn, September 15, 2016, https://www.linkedin.com/pulse/lead-acknowledge-what-you-dont-know-geoffrey-garrett.

2. R. Mehra, "Global Public Health Problem of Sudden Cardiac Death," *Journal of Electrocardiology* 40, no. 6 (2007): S118–S122.

3. This section draws on J. P. Ackerman et al., "The Promise and Peril of Precision Medicine," *Mayo Clinic Proceedings* 91, no. 11 (2016):

1606–1616, and R. Winslow, "Boy's Cardiac Death Led to Misuse of Genetic Test, Study Says," *Wall Street Journal*, October 21, 2016.

4. H. Singh, A. N. D. Meyer, and E. J. Thomas, "The Frequency of Diagnostic Errors in Outpatient Care: Estimations from Three Large Observational Studies Involving US Adult Populations," *BMJ Quality and Safety* 23, no. 9 (2014): 727–731.

5. T. Pohlmann and N. M. Thomas, "Relearning the Art of Asking Questions," *Harvard Business Review*, March 27, 2015.

6. *Discovery and Development of Penicillin* (London: Alexander Fleming Laboratory Museum, 1999).

7. American Chemistry Society, "Edwin Land and Polaroid Photography," http://www.acs.org/content/acs/en/education/whatischemistry/landmarks/land-instant-photography.html.

8. F. Gino and B. R. Staats, "Mary Caroline Tillman at Egon Zehnder: Spotting Talent in the 21st Century," Case 416-017 (Boston: Harvard Business School Publishing, 2015).

9. M. Goldsmith, *What Got You Here Won't Get You There: How Successful People Become Even More Successful* (New York: Hyperion, 2007).

10. T. B. Kashdan, R. A. Sherman, J. Yarbro, and D. C. Funder, "How Are Curious People Viewed and How Do They Behave in Social Situations? From the Perspectives of Self, Friends, Parents, and Unacquainted Observers," *Journal of Personality* 81, no. 2 (2013): 142–154. For related work, see G. Loewenstein, "The Psychology of Curiosity: A Review and Reinterpretation," *Psychological Bulletin* 116, no. 1 (1994): 75–98; and T. B. Kashdan, P. Rose, and F. D. Fincham, "Curiosity and Exploration: Facilitating Positive Subjective Experiences and Personal Growth Opportunities," *Journal of Personality Assessment* 82, no. 3 (2004): 291–305.

11. K. Huang et al., "It Doesn't Hurt to Ask: Question-Asking Increases Liking," *Journal of Personality and Social Psychology* 113, no. 3 (September 2017): 430–452.

12. T. B. Kashdan and M. F. Steger, "Curiosity and Pathways to Well-Being and Meaning in Life: Traits, States, and Everyday Behaviors," *Motivation and Emotion* 31 (2007): 159–173; and T. B. Kashdan and J. Rottenberg, "Psychological Flexibility as a Fundamental Aspect of Health," *Clinical Psychology Review* 30 (2010): 865–878.

13. "DoD News Briefing—Secretary Rumsfeld and Gen. Myers," US Department of Defense, February 12, 2002, http://archive.defense.gov/Transcripts/Transcript.aspx?TranscriptID=2636.

14. Or try this link: https://www.youtube.com/watch?v=vJG698U2Mvo.

15. D. J. Simons and C. F. Chabris, "Gorillas in Our Midst: Sustained Inattentional Blindness for Dynamic Events," *Perception* 28, no. 9 (1999): 1059–1074.

16. U. Neisser, *The Control of Information Pickup in Selective Looking. Perception and Its Development: A Tribute to Eleanor J. Gibson*, ed. A. D. Pick (Hillsdale, NJ: Lawrence Erlbaum Associates, 1979).

17. D. J. Simons, "Monkeying Around with the Gorillas in Our Midst: Familiarity with an Inattentional-Blindness Task Does Not Improve the Detection of Unexpected Events," *i-Perception* 1, no. 1 (2010): 3–6.

18. A. Tversky and D. Kahneman, "Availability: A Heuristic for Judging Frequency and Probability," *Cognitive Psychology* 5, no. 2 (1973): 207–232; and C. MacLeod and L. Campbell, "Memory Accessibility and Probability Judgments: An Experimental Evaluation of the Availability Heuristic," *Journal of Personality and Social Psychology* 63, no. 6 (1992): 890–902.

19. E. Bakshy, S. Messing, and L. A. Adamic, "Exposure to Ideologically Diverse News and Opinion on Facebook," *Science* 348, no. 6239 (2015): 1130–1132.

20. A final reason this occurs is that Facebook uses algorithms to push articles to users. Despite Facebook's initial claims to the contrary, those algorithms also help produce the echo chamber effect (Z. Tufekci, "Facebook Said Its Algorithms Do Help Form Echo Chambers, and the Tech Press Missed It," *New Perspectives Quarterly* 32, no. 3 [2015]: 9–12; and K. Hosanagar, "Blame the Echo Chamber on Facebook. But Blame Yourself, Too," *Wired*, November 25, 2016). See Zeynep Tufekci's broader work for an interesting discussion of the way algorithms shape how we see the world more broadly: https://sils.unc.edu/people/faculty/zeynep-tufekci.

21. B. Bishop, *The Big Sort: Why the Clustering of Like-Minded America Is Tearing Us Apart* (Boston: Houghton Mifflin Harcourt, 2009).

22. T. B. Lee, "Facebook's Fake News Problem, Explained," *Vox*, November 16, 2016.

23. P. Green, F. Gino, and B. R. Staats, "Shopping for Confirmation: How Threatening Feedback Leads People to Reshape Their Social Networks," working paper 18-028, Harvard Business School, Boston, 2016.

24. M. Snyder and J. A. Haugen, "Why Does Behavioral Confirmation Occur? A Functional Perspective on the Role of the Perceiver," *Journal of Experimental Social Psychology* 30, no. 3 (1994): 218–246; and M. Snyder and J. A. Haugen, "Why Does Behavioral Confirmation Occur? A Functional Perspective on the Role of the Target," *Personality and Social Psychology Bulletin* 21, no. 9 (1995): 963–974.

25. M. H. Bazerman and D. Chugh, "Decisions Without Blinders," *Harvard Business Review* 84, no. 1 (2006): 88.

26. H. D. Thoreau, *Walden* (Boston: Houghton Mifflin, 1906).

27. See http://bobsutton.typepad.com/my_weblog/2006/07/strong_opinions.html.

28. D. Lovallo and D. Kahneman, "Delusions of Success," *Harvard Business Review* 81, no. 7 (2003): 56–63.

29. Another common way of demonstrating this in business school classes is the 2-4-6 exercise (Bazerman and Chugh, "Decisions Without Blinders"). In this exercise, I show students the numbers 2, 4, and 6 and ask them to identify the relationships among the three. They can then show me three numbers, and I will tell them whether their numbers match the rule. When they're ready, they can guess the rule. Typically

people will guess a pattern of increasing even numbers (say, 6-8-10) or of increases by two (say, 1-3-5). They look to confirm their initial perspective. As before, the proper approach would be to reject alternatives to reveal the true rule: any three increasing numbers.

30. L. Ross, D. Greene, and P. House, "The 'False Consensus Effect': An Egocentric Bias in Social Perception and Attribution Processes," *Journal of Experimental Social Psychology* 13, no. 3 (1977): 279–301.

31. This is hard to do. The best solution I've found is to leave the tempting device behind—or at the very least, deep in your pocket.

Chapter 5

1. A. Fifield, "Do the Japanese Really Work Themselves to Death? In Some Cases, Yes," *Washington Post*, July 31, 2016.

2. Ibid.

3. Ibid.

4. K. Spitzer, "Japanese Are Working Themselves to Death— Literally," *USA Today*, October 17, 2016.

5. Fifield, "Do the Japanese Really Work Themselves to Death?"

6. D. M. Upton and B. R. Staats, "Radically Simple IT," *Harvard Business Review* 86, no. 3 (2008): 118–124.

7. "A Culture of Think," IBM, accessed November 7, 2017, from http://www-03.ibm.com/ibm/history/ibm100/us/en/icons/think_culture/.

8. These are often referred to as System 1 and System 2—perhaps low on creativity, but easy to distinguish. D. Kahneman, *Thinking, Fast and Slow* (New York: Farrar, Straus & Giroux, 2011); and J. Evans and K. Stanovich, "Dual-Process Theories of Higher Cognition: Advancing the Debate," *Perspectives on Psychological Science* 8, no. 3 (2013): 223–241.

9. C. Argyris, "Double Loop Learning in Organizations," *Harvard Business Review* 55, no. 5 (1977): 115–124; C. Argyris and D. A. Schön, *Organizational Learning* (Reading, MA: Addison-Wesley, 1978); and C. Argyris, *On Organizational Learning* (Oxford: Blackwell Business, 1999).

10. L. Nyberg et al., "Learning by Doing versus Learning by Thinking: An fMRI Study of Motor and Mental Training," *Neuropsychologia* 44, no. 5 (2006): 711–717; C.-J. Olsson, B. Jonsson, and L. Nyberg, "Learning by Doing and Learning by Thinking: An fMRI Study of Combining Motor and Mental Training," *Frontiers in Human Neuroscience* 2 (2008): 5; M. H. Immordino-Yang, J. A. Christodoulou, and V. Singh, "Rest Is Not Idleness: Implications of the Brain's Default Mode for Human Development and Education," *Perspectives on Psychological Science* 7, no. 4 (2012): 352–364; and A. Saimpont et al., "The Comparison between Motor Imagery and Verbal Rehearsal on the Learning of Sequential Movements," *Frontiers in Human Neuroscience* 7 (2013): 1–9.

11. A. Bandura, *Self-Efficacy in Changing Societies* (Cambridge: Cambridge University Press, 1995), 2.

12. R. White, "Motivation Reconsidered: The Concept of Competence," *Psychological Review* 66 (1959): 297–333; and R. M. Ryan and E. L. Deci, "Self-Determination Theory and the Facilitation of Intrinsic Motivation, Social Development, and Well-Being," *American Psychologist* 55 (2000): 68–78.

13. A. Bandura, *Social Foundations of Thought and Action: A Social Cognitive Theory* (Englewood Cliffs, NJ: Prentice-Hall, 1986); S. Taylor, "Asymmetrical Effects of Positive and Negative Events: The Mobilization/ Minimization Hypothesis," *Psychological Bulletin* 110 (1991): 67–85.

14. G. Di Stefano et al., "Under a Magnifying Glass: Understanding the Microfoundations of Organizational Learning," working paper, Harvard Business School, Boston, 2016.

15. M. Bar-Eli et al., "Action Bias among Elite Soccer Goalkeepers: The Case of Penalty Kicks," *Journal of Economic Psychology* 28, no. 5 (2007): 606–621.

16. K. D. Elsbach, D. M. Cable, and J. W. Sherman, "How Passive 'Face Time' Affects Perceptions of Employees: Evidence of Spontaneous Trait Inference," *Human Relations* 63, no. 6 (2010): 735–760; and K. Elsbach and D. Cable, "Why Showing Your Face at Work Matters," *MIT Sloan Management Review* 53, no. 4 (2012): 10–12.

17. Interestingly, these results did not hold in similar studies with Italian participants, in which leisure was viewed as a sign of status. S. Bellezza, A. Keinan, and N. Paharia, "Conspicuous Consumption of Time: When Busyness and Lack of Leisure Time Become a Status Symbol," *NA-Advances in Consumer Research* 42 (2014); and S. Bellezza, A. Keinan, and N. Paharia, "Research: Why Americans Are So Impressed by Busyness," *Harvard Business Review*, December 15, 2016.

18. E. Reid, "Why Some Men Pretend to Work 80-Hour Weeks," *Harvard Business Review*, April 28, 2015.

19. Bar-Eli, "Action Bias among Elite Soccer Goalkeepers."

20. T. Amabile and S. Kramer, *The Progress Principle: Using Small Wins to Ignite Joy, Engagement, and Creativity at Work* (Boston: Harvard Business Review Press, 2011).

21. T. M. Amabile et al., "Leader Behaviors and the Work Environment for Creativity: Perceived Leader Support," *Leadership Quarterly* 15, no. 1 (2004): 5–32; and T. M. Amabile et al., "Affect and Creativity at Work," *Administrative Science Quarterly* 50, no. 3 (2005): 367–403.

22. M. Amar et al., "Winning the Battle but Losing the War: The Psychology of Debt Management," *Journal of Marketing Research* 48 (2011): S38–S50.

23. D. KC and C. Terwiesch, "Impact of Workload on Service Time and Patient Safety: An Econometric Analysis of Hospital Operations," *Management Science* 55, no. 9 (2009): 1486–1498. See also K. L. Schultz, D. C. Juran, and J. W. Boudreau, "The Effects of Low Inventory on the Development of Productivity Norms," *Management Science* 45, no. 12 (1999): 1664–1678.

24. B. R. Staats and F. Gino, "Specialization and Variety in Repetitive Tasks: Evidence from a Japanese Bank," *Management Science* 58, no. 6 (2012): 1141–1159; and L. Kuntz, R. Mennicken, and S. Scholtes, "Stress on the Ward: Evidence of Safety Tipping Points in Hospitals," *Management Science* 61, no. 4 (2014): 754–771.

25. H. Dai et al., "The Impact of Time at Work and Time Off from Work on Rule Compliance: The Case of Hand Hygiene in Health Care," *Journal of Applied Psychology* 100, no. 3 (2015): 846; and B. R. Staats, H. Dai, and K. L. Milkman, "Motivating Process Compliance through Individual Electronic Monitoring: An Empirical Examination of Hand Hygiene in Healthcare," *Management Science* 63, no. 5 (2016): 1563–1585.

26. M. S. Christian and A. P. J. Ellis, "Examining the Effects of Sleep Deprivation on Workplace Deviance: A Self-Regulatory Perspective," *Academy of Management Journal* 54, no. 5 (2011): 913–934; and S. G. Carmichael, "The Research Is Clear: Long Hours Backfire for People and for Companies," *Harvard Business Review*, August 19, 2015, https://hbr.org/2015/08/the-research-is-clear-long-hours-backfire-for-people-and-for-companies.

27. A. L. Tucker, A. C. Edmondson, and S. Spear, "When Problem Solving Prevents Organizational Learning," *Journal of Organizational Change Management* 15, no. 2 (2002): 122; A. L. Tucker, "The Impact of Operational Failures on Hospital Nurses and Their Patients," *Journal of Operations Management* 22, no. 2 (2004): 151; and A. L. Tucker, "The Impact of Workaround Difficulty on Frontline Employees' Response to Operational Failures: A Laboratory Experiment on Medication Administration," *Management Science* 62, no. 4 (2015).

28. P. Pendem et al., "The Microstructure of Work: How Unexpected Breaks Let You Rest, but Not Lose Focus," working paper 17-058, Harvard Business School, Boston, 2016.

29. T. Belden and M. Belden, *The Lengthening Shadow: The Life of Thomas J. Watson* (New York: Little, Brown and Company, 1962), 157–158.

30. M. C. Schippers, A. C. Homan, and D. Knippenberg, "To Reflect or Not to Reflect: Prior Team Performance as a Boundary Condition of the Effects of Reflexivity on Learning and Final Team Performance," *Journal of Organizational Behavior* 34, no. 1 (2013): 6–23; and M. C. Schippers, A. C. Edmondson, and M. A. West, "Team Reflexivity as an Antidote to Team Information-Processing Failures," *Small Group Research* 45, no. 6 (2014): 731–769.

31. D. Burkus, "The Creative Benefits of Boredom," *Harvard Business Review*, September 9, 2014; and K. Gasper and B. L. Middlewood, "Approaching Novel Thoughts: Understanding Why Elation and Boredom Promote Associative Thought More Than Distress and Relaxation," *Journal of Experimental Social Psychology* 52 (2014): 50–57; and S. Mann and R. Cadman, "Does Being Bored Make Us More Creative?" *Creativity Research Journal* 26, no. 2 (2014): 165–173.

32. G. Klein, "Performing a Project Premortem," *Harvard Business Review* 85, no. 9 (2007): 18–19.

33. J. E. Morrison and L. L. Meliza, "Foundations of the After Action Review Process," DTIC document, 1999; K. Walshe, "Understanding and Learning from Organisational Failure," *Quality and Safety in Health Care* 12, no. 2 (2003): 81–82; S. Ellis and I. Davidi, "After-Event Reviews: Drawing Lessons from Successful and Failed Experience," *Journal of Applied Psychology* 90, no. 5 (2005): 857; E. W. Rogers and J. Milam, "Pausing for Learning: Applying the After Action Review Process at the NASA Goddard Space Flight Center," IEEE, 2005 IEEE Aerospace Conference; E. Catmull, *Creativity, Inc.: Overcoming the Unseen Forces That Stand in the Way of True Inspiration* (New York: Random House, 2014); and D. A. Katz et al., "Using Serious Gaming to Improve the Safety of Central Venous Catheter Placement: A Post-Mortem Analysis," *International Journal of Gaming and Computer-Mediated Simulations* 6, no. 4 (2014): 34–44.

34. To name just a few: P. Lavie, J. Zomer, and D. Gopher, "Ultradian Rhythms in Prolonged Human Performance," ARI research note 95-30, 1995; A. Ariga and A. Lleras, "Brief and Rare Mental 'Breaks' Keep You Focused: Deactivation and Reactivation of Task Goals Preempt Vigilance Decrements," *Cognition* 118, no. 3 (2011): 439–443; F. Cirillo, *The Pomodoro Technique* (New York: Simon & Schuster, 2014); and D. Thompson, "A Formula for Perfect Productivity: Work for 52 Minutes, Break for 17," *The Atlantic*, September 17, 2014.

35. Cirillo, *The Pomodoro Technique*.

36. J. P. Trougakos et al., "Making the Break Count: An Episodic Examination of Recovery Activities, Emotional Experiences, and Positive Affective Displays," *Academy of Management Journal* 51, no. 1 (2008): 131–146; R. M. Ryan et al., "Vitalizing Effects of Being Outdoors and in Nature," *Journal of Environmental Psychology* 30, no. 2 (2010): 159–168; L. Tyrväinen et al., "The Influence of Urban Green Environments on Stress Relief Measures: A Field Experiment," *Journal of Environmental Psychology* 38 (2014): 1–9; G. N. Bratman et al., "The Benefits of Nature Experience: Improved Affect and Cognition," *Landscape and Urban Planning* 138 (2015): 41–50; S. Kim, Y. Park, and Q. Niu, "Micro-Break Activities at Work to Recover from Daily Work Demands," *Journal of Organizational Behavior* 38, no. 1 (2017); and H. Rhee and S. Kim, "Effects of Breaks on Regaining Vitality at Work: An Empirical Comparison of 'Conventional' and 'Smart Phone' Breaks," *Computers in Human Behavior* 57 (2016): 160–167.

37. L. F. ten Brinke et al., "Aerobic Exercise Increases Hippocampal Volume in Older Women with Probable Mild Cognitive Impairment: A 6-Month Randomised Controlled Trial," *British Journal of Sports Medicine* 49, no. 4 (2014).

38. H. Dai et al., "The Impact of Time at Work and Time Off from Work on Rule Compliance: The Case of Hand Hygiene in Health Care," *Journal of Applied Psychology* 100, no. 3 (2015): 846.

39. A. Huffington, *Thrive: The Third Metric to Redefining Success and Creating a Happier Life* (New York: Random House, 2014); and C. M. Barnes and G. Spreitzer, "Why Sleep Is a Strategic Resource," *MIT Sloan Management Review* 56, no. 2 (2015): 19.

40. D. Thompson, "Why Summer Vacations (and the Internet) Make You More Productive," *The Atlantic*, August 29, 2011.

41. The late and great Richard Hackman discussed this with respect to team leaders setting up conditions for success for their teams. This is a slight shift of that message to think about time. J. R. Hackman, *Leading Teams: Setting the Stage for Great Performances* (Boston: Harvard Business School Press, 2002).

42. N. Bloom et al., "Does Working from Home Work? Evidence from a Chinese Experiment," *Quarterly Journal of Economics* 130, no. 1 (2015): 165–218.

Chapter 6

1. B. Potter, *The Tale of Peter Rabbit* (London: Frederick Warne & Co., 1902; Project Gutenberg, 2005).

2. F. Gino and B. R. Staats, "Samasource: Give Work Not Aid," Case 912-011 (Boston: Harvard Business School Publishing, 2011).

3. Ibid.

4. See www.lxmi.com. For more of Leila's story, see L. Janah, *Give Work: Reversing Poverty One Job at a Time* (New York: Penguin Random House, 2017).

15. F. W. Taylor, *The Principles of Scientific Management* (New York: Harper & Brothers, 1911); F. Herzberg, "One More Time: How Do You Motivate Employees?" *Harvard Business Review* 46, no. 1 (1968): 53–62; J. R. Hackman and G. R. Oldham, "Motivation Through the Design of Work: Test of a Theory," *Organizational Behavior and Human Performance* 16, no. 2 (1976): 250–279; J. R. Hackman and G. R. Oldham, *Work Redesign* (Reading, MA: Addison-Wesley, 1980); J. Cameron and W. D. Pierce, "Reinforcement, Reward, and Intrinsic Motivation: A Meta-Analysis," *Review of Educational Research* 64, no. 3 (1994): 363–423; E. L. Deci and R. M. Ryan, "A Meta-Analytic Review of Experiments Examining the Effects of Extrinsic Rewards on Intrinsic Motivation," *Psychological Bulletin* 125, no. 6 (1999): 627–668; R. M. Ryan and E. L. Deci, "Self-Determination Theory and the Facilitation of Intrinsic Motivation, Social Development, and Well-Being," *American Psychologist* 55 (2000): 68–78; and M. Gagné and E. L. Deci, "Self-Determination Theory and Work Motivation," *Journal of Organizational Behavior* 26, no. 4 (2005): 331–362.

6. Herzberg, "One More Time."

7. Ibid., 88.

8. M. H. Kernis, "Toward a Conceptualization of Optimal Self-Esteem," *Psychological Inquiry* 14 (2003): 1–26; C. Guignon, *On Being Authentic* (New York: Routledge, 2004); M. E. P. Seligman et al., "Positive Psychology Progress: Empirical Validation of Interventions," *American Psychologist* 60 (2005): 410–421; D. M. Cable, F. Gino, and B. R. Staats, "Breaking Them In or Revealing Their Best? Reframing Socialization Around Newcomer Self Expression," *Administrative Science Quarterly* 58, no. 1 (2013): 1–36.

9. B. L. Fredrickson, "What Good Are Positive Emotions?" *Review of General Psychology* 2, no. 3 (1998): 300; B. L. Fredrickson, "The Role of Positive Emotions in Positive Psychology: The Broaden-and-Build Theory of Positive Emotions," *American Psychologist* 56, no. 3 (2001): 218; and B. Fredrickson, *Positivity* (New York: Harmony Books, 2009).

10. H. A. Wadlinger and D. M. Isaacowitz, "Positive Mood Broadens Visual Attention to Positive Stimuli," *Motivation and Emotion* 30, no. 1 (2006): 87–99; G. Rowe, J. B. Hirsh, and A. K. Anderson, "Positive Affect Increases the Breadth of Attentional Selection," *Proceedings of the National Academy of Sciences* 104, no. 1 (2007): 383–388; T. W. Schmitz, E. De Rosa, and A. K. Anderson, "Opposing Influences of Affective State Valence on Visual Cortical Encoding," *Journal of Neuroscience* 29, no. 22 (2009): 7199–7207; and B. L. Fredrickson, "Updated Thinking on Positivity Ratios," *American Psychology* 68, no. 9 (2013): 814–822.

11. B. L. Fredrickson et al., "Open Hearts Build Lives: Positive Emotions, Induced Through Loving-Kindness Meditation, Build Consequential Personal Resources," *Journal of Personality and Social Psychology* 95, no. 5 (2008): 1045; L. Sekerka, T. Vacharkulksemsuk, and B. Fredrickson, "Positive Emotions: Broadening-and-Building Upward Spirals of Sustainable Development" in *The Oxford Handbook of Positive Organizational Scholarship*; eds. G. M. Spreitzer and K. S. Cameron (Oxford: Oxford University Press, 2012), 168–177; B. E. Kok et al., "How Positive Emotions Build Physical Health: Perceived Positive Social Connections Account for the Upward Spiral Between Positive Emotions and Vagal Tone," *Psychological Science* 24, no. 7 (2013): 1123–1132.

12. You can take a survey created by Dr. Clance to evaluate where you fall on the impostor syndrome by going to http://paulineroseclance.com/pdf/IPTestandscoring.pdf. P. R. Clance and S. A. Imes, "The Impostor Phenomenon in High Achieving Women: Dynamics and Therapeutic Interventions," *Psychotherapy: Theory Research and Practice* 15 (1978): 241–247; and P. R. Clance, *The Impostor Phenomenon: When Success Makes You Feel Like a Fake* (New York: Bantam Books, 1985).

13. C. Richards, "Learning to Deal with the Impostor Syndrome," *New York Times*, October 26, 2015.

14. R. Jones, "What CEOs Are Afraid Of," *Harvard Business Review*, February 24, 2015.

15. S. E. Asch, "Effects of Group Pressure upon the Modification and Distortion of Judgments," *Groups, Leadership, and Men* (spring 1951): 222–236; S. E. Asch, "Studies of Independence and Conformity: I. A Minority of One Against a Unanimous Majority," *Psychological Monographs: General and Applied* 70, no. 9 (1956): 1; and R. B. Cialdini and M. R. Trost, "Social Influence: Social Norms, Conformity and Compliance," in *The Handbook of Social Psychology*, eds. D. T. Gilbert et al. (New York: Wiley, 1998).

16. A. A. Grandey, "When 'The Show Must Go On': Surface Acting and Deep Acting as Determinants of Emotional Exhaustion and Peer-Rated Service Delivery," *Academy of Management Journal* 46, no. 1 (2003):

86–96; M. E. P. Seligman et al., "Positive Psychology Progress: Empirical Validation of Interventions," *American Psychologist* 60 (2005): 410–421; and S. Melamed et al., "Burnout and Risk of Cardiovascular Disease: Evidence, Possible Causal Paths, and Promising Research Directions," *Psychological Bulletin* 132, no. 3 (2006): 327.

17. R. M. Yerkes and J. D. Dodson, "The Relation of Strength of Stimulus to Rapidity of Habit Formation," *Journal of Comparative Neurology and Psychology* 18, no. 5 (1908): 459–482; and K. H. Teigen, "Yerkes-Dodson: A Law for All Seasons," *Theory and Psychology* 4, no. 4 (1994): 525–547.

18. B. M. Staw, L. E. Sandelands, and J. E. Dutton, "Threat Rigidity Effects in Organizational Behavior: A Multilevel Analysis," *Administrative Science Quarterly* 26, no. 4 (1981): 501–524; C. Gilbert, "Unbundling the Structure of Inertia: Resource vs. Routine Rigidity," *Academy of Management Journal* 48, no. 5 (2005): 741–763; and C. Gilbert, "Change in the Presence of Residual Fit: Can Competing Frames Coexist?" *Organization Science* 17, no. 1 (2006): 150–167.

19. We also included an additional treatment that individuals went through in teams. Performance on the team treatment was no different, statistically, from performance on the organizational treatment.

20. *The Breakfast Club*, directed by J. Hughes (Universal City, CA: Universal Pictures, 1985).

21. M. B. Brewer and R. M. Kramer, "Choice Behavior in Social Dilemmas: Effects of Social Identity, Group Size, and Decision Framing," *Journal of Personality and Social Psychology* 50, no. 3 (1986): 543–549; M. B. Brewer and W. Gardner, "Who Is This 'We'? Levels of Collective Identity and Self Representations," *Journal of Personality and Social Psychology* 71, no. 1 (1996): 83–93; and A. Goldberg et al., "Fitting In or Standing Out? The Tradeoffs of Structural and Cultural Embeddedness," *American Sociological Review* 81, no. 6 (2016): 1190–1222.

22. S. F. Bellezza, F. Gino, and A. Keinan, "The Red Sneakers Effect: Inferring Status and Competence from Signals of Nonconformity," *Journal of Consumer Research* 41, no. 1 (2014): 35–54.

23. T. B. Bitterly, A. W. Brooks, and M. E. Schweitzer, "Risky Business: When Humor Increases and Decreases Status," *Journal of Personality and Social Psychology* 112, no. 3 (2017): 431–455.

24. E. W. Dunn, L. B. Aknin, and M. I. Norton, "Spending Money on Others Promotes Happiness," *Science* 319, no. 5870 (2008): 1687–1688.

25. B. Sutton, "The Best You Can Be Is a Perfect Imitation of Those Who Came Before You," *Medium*, December 10, 2016, https://medium.com/@bobsutton/the-best-you-can-be-is-a-perfect-imitation-of-those-who-came-before-you-e580b49c7ca0.

Chapter 7

1. F. Herzberg, "One More Time: How Do You Motivate Employees?" *Harvard Business Review* 46, no. 1 (1968): 53–62; and G. R. Oldham and J. R. Hackman, "Not What It Was and Not What It Will Be: The Future of Job Design Research," *Journal of Organizational Behavior* 31, no. 2 (2010): 463–479.

2. D. M. Lawson, *Posterity: Letters of Great Americans to Their Children* (New York: Anchor Books, 2008).

3. T. S. Amabile and S. Kramer, *The Progress Principle: Using Small Wins to Ignite Joy, Engagement, and Creativity at Work* (Boston: Harvard Business Review Press, 2011).

4. B. Rigoni and B. Nelson, "Do Employees Really Know What's Expected of Them?" Gallup, September 27, 2016.

5. J. A. Lee et al., "Best-Self Activation Improves Emotions, Physiology, and Problem Solving," working paper, Harvard Business School, Boston, 2017.

6. I. Larkin, "Paying $30,000 for a Gold Star: An Empirical Investigation into the Value of Peer Recognition to Software Salespeople," working paper, Harvard Business School, Boston, 2012.

7. Rigoni, "Do Employees Really Know What's Expected of Them?"

8. Ibid.

9. If you want to laugh, then spend some time at Tom's website: https:// marketoonist.com/. Tom is a great example of someone who uses his strengths to learn. He was my section mate at HBS. When he was there, he discovered both a love and a talent for drawing cartoons—https:// marketoonist.com/skydeckyear1. He didn't pursue this passion right away; instead he followed the path of a marketer. But he continued to parody what he was seeing until he realized that he could take the leap and strike out on his own. Now, he keeps us all entertained, and himself happy and economically content, and he is learning constantly through his art and study of business.

10. T. Hill, *Manufacturing Strategy: Text and Cases* (Blue Ridge, Ill.: McGraw-Hill/Irwin, 1993).

11. C. Board, *Student Descriptive Questionnaire* (Princeton, NJ: Educational Testing Service, 1976–1977).

12. N. Epley and D. Dunning, "Feeling 'Holier Than Thou': Are Self-Serving Assessments Produced by Errors in Self- or Social Prediction?" *Journal of Personality and Social Psychology* 79, no. 6 (2000): 861–875.

13. D. Dunning, C. Heath, and J. M. Suls, "Flawed Self-Assessment Implications for Health, Education, and the Workplace," *Psychological Science in the Public Interest* 5, no. 3 (2004): 69–106.

14. H. H. Meyer, "Self-Appraisal of Job Performance," *Personnel Psychology* 33, no. 2 (1980): 291–295.

15. J. A. Lee et al., "Bringing Employees' Best Selves to Employment Relationships Reduces Burnout," working paper, Harvard Business School, Boston, 2016.

16. L. M. Roberts et al., "How to Play to Your Strengths," *Harvard Business Review* 83, no. 1 (2005).

17. Co-owned by my colleague Dan Cable.

18. L. Lee, "Should Employees Design Their Own Jobs?" *Insights by Stanford Business*, January 22, 2016.

19. Hill, *Manufacturing Strategy*.

20. This is a good time to point out that although I saw the fit, I don't think I did a particularly good job of communicating that. However, both David Upton and Ananth Raman saw something that each, in his own way, was willing to bet on and then develop. A thank-you here is insufficient but most appropriate.

21. As quoted in N. Trautmann, "The Dose Makes the Poison—or Does It?" Action Bioscience, January 2005, www.actionbioscience.org/environment/trautmann.html.

22. F. Street, "The Value of Grey Thinking," Farnam Street blog, 2016, https://www.farnamstreetblog.com/about/.

23. B. R. Staats, D. KC, and F. Gino, "Maintaining Beliefs in the Face of Negative News: The Moderating Role of Experience," *Management Science* (forthcoming 2017).

Chapter 8

1. L. S. Vygotsky, *Mind in Society: The Development of Higher Psychological Processes* (Cambridge, MA: Harvard University Press, 1978).

2. Ibid.

3. Ibid.

4. A. Smith, *An Inquiry into the Nature and Causes of the Wealth of Nations* (London: W. Strahan and T. Cadell, 1776).

5. T. P. Wright, "Factors Affecting the Cost of Airplanes," *Journal of Aeronautical Science* 3 (1936): 122–128; E. D. Darr and D. Epple, "The Acquisition, Transfer, and Depreciation of Knowledge in Service Organizations: Productivity in Franchises," *Management Science* 41, no. 11 (1995): 1750–1762; L. Argote, *Organizational Learning: Creating, Retaining, and Transferring Knowledge* (Boston: Kluwer Academic, 1999); G. P. Pisano et al., "Organizational Differences in Rates of Learning: Evidence from the Adoption of Minimally Invasive Cardiac Surgery," *Management Science* 47, no. 6 (2001): 752–768; P. Ingram and T. Simons, "The Transfer of Experience in Groups of Organizations: Implications for Performance and Competition," *Management Science* 48, no. 12 (2002): 1517–1533; R. Reagans, L. Argote, and D. Brooks, "Individual Experience and Experience Working Together," *Management Science* 51, no. 6 (2005): 869–881; and M. A. Lapré and N. Tsikriktsis, "Organizational Learning Curves for Customer Dissatisfaction: Heterogeneity Across Airlines," *Management Science* 52, no. 3 (2006): 352–366.

6. P. B. Kantor and W. I. Zangwill, "Theoretical Foundation for a Learning Rate Budget," *Management Science* 37, no. 3 (1991): 315–330; and W. I. Zangwill and P. B. Kantor, "Toward a Theory of Continuous Improvement and the Learning Curve," *Management Science* 44, no. 7 (1998): 910–920.

7. J. R. Clark, R. S. Huckman, and B. R. Staats, "Customer Specificity and Learning: Evidence from Outsourced Radiological Services," *Organization Science* 24, no. 5 (2013): 1539–1557.

8. In 2002 a psychologist, Daniel Kahneman, was awarded the Nobel Prize in Economics for his work showing that even assumptions of rationality could be wrong.

9. A. Hargadon and R. I. Sutton, "Technology Brokering and Innovation in a Product Development Firm," *Administrative Science Quarterly* 42, no. 4 (1997): 716–749.

10. K. R. Lakhani and L. B. Jeppesen, "Getting Unusual Suspects to Solve R&D Puzzles," *Harvard Business Review* 85, no. 5 (2007): 30–32.

11. J. A. Schumpeter, *The Theory of Economic Development: An Inquiry into Profits, Capital, Credit, Interest, and the Business Cycle* (New Brunswick, NJ: Transaction Books, 1934).

12. R. Derfler-Rozin, C. Moore, and B. R. Staats, "Reducing Organizational Rule Breaking Through Task Variety," *Organization Science* 27, no. 6 (2016): 1361–1379.

13. F. J. Roethlisberger and W. J. Dickson, *Management and the Worker* (Boston: Harvard University Press, 1934); and D. F. Roy, "'Banana Time': Job Satisfaction and Informal Interaction," *Human Organization* 18, no. 4 (1959): 158–168.

14. B. M. Staw, "Knee-Deep in the Big Muddy: A Study of Escalating Commitment to a Chosen Course of Action," *Organizational Behavior and Human Decision Processes* 16, no. 1 (1976): 27–44; and D. J. Sleesman et al., "Cleaning Up the Big Muddy: A Meta-Analytic Review of the Determinants of Escalation of Commitment," *Academy of Management Journal* 55, no. 3 (2012): 541–562.

15. B. R. Staats, D. KC, and F. Gino, "Maintaining Beliefs in the Face of Negative News: The Moderating Role of Experience," *Management Science* (forthcoming 2017).

16. R. F. Scott and L. Huxley, *Scott's Last Expedition, Volume I: Being the Journals of Captain R. F. Scott, R.N., C.V.O.* (London: Smith, Elder & Co., 1913), 369.

17. D. KC and B. R. Staats, "Accumulating a Portfolio of Experience: The Effect of Focal and Related Experience on Surgeon Performance," *Manufacturing and Service Operations Management* 14, no. 4 (2012): 618–633.

18. R. D. Rogers and S. Monsell, "Costs of a Predictable Switch Between Simple Cognitive Tasks," *Journal of Experimental Psychology* 124, no. 2 (1995): 207–231; A. Allport and G. Wylie, "Task-Switching, Stimulus-Response Bindings and Negative Priming," in *Control of Cognitive Processes: Attention and Performance*, vol. XVIII, eds. S. Monsell and J. Driver (Cambridge, MA: MIT Press, 2000), 35–70; and S. Monsell, "Task Switching," *Trends in Cognitive Sciences* 7, no. 3 (2003): 134–140.

19. J. S. Rubinstein, D. E. Meyer, and J. E. Evans, "Executive Control of Cognitive Processes in Task Switching," *Journal of Experimental Psychology: Human Perception and Performance* 27, no. 4 (2001): 763.

20. Rogers, "Costs of a Predictable Switch Between Simple Cognitive Tasks"; and Allport, "Task-Switching, Stimulus-Response Bindings, and Negative Priming."

21. G. Wylie and A. Allport, "Task Switching and the Measurement of Switch Costs," *Psychological Research* 63, no. 3-4 (2000): 212–233; and F. Waszak, B. Hommel, and A. Allport, "Task-Switching and Long-Term Priming: Role of Episodic Stimulus-Task Bindings in Task-Shift Costs," *Cognitive Psychology* 46, no. 4 (2003): 361–413.

22. Rogers, "Costs of a Predictable Switch Between Simple Cognitive Tasks"; and S. Monsell, "Task Switching," *Trends in Cognitive Sciences* 7, no. 3 (2003): 134–140.

23. B. R. Staats and F. Gino, "Specialization and Variety in Repetitive Tasks: Evidence from a Japanese Bank," *Management Science* 58, no. 6 (2012): 1141–1159.

24. For those interested in important concerns such as empirical identification, variety was assigned by an algorithm in the bank's computer system. The algorithm sought to give workers the same task repeatedly; however, if another task was backed up, they would be switched dynamically.

25. See http://steamspy.com/.

26. This section draws on E. S. Bernstein, F. Gino, and B. R. Staats, "Opening the Valve: From Software to Hardware (A)," Case 9-415-015 (Boston: Harvard Business School Publishing, 2014).

27. Valve, "Valve: Handbook for New Employees," 2012: 39.

28. Ibid., 46.

29. R. W. Buell, R. S. Huckman, and S. Travers, "Improving Access at VA," Case 9-617-012 (Boston: Harvard Business School, 2016): 6.

30. Ibid.

31. Ibid, 5.

32. Ibid.

33. Ibid., 8

34. D. J. Brunner et al., "Wellsprings of Creation: How Perturbation Sustains Exploration in Mature Organizations," working paper 09-011, Harvard Business School, Boston, 2009.

35. M. A. Schilling et al., "Learning by Doing Something Else: Variation, Relatedness, and the Learning Curve," *Management Science* 49, no. 1 (2003): 39–56; J. R. Clark and R. S. Huckman, "Broadening Focus: Spillovers and the Benefits of Specialization in the Hospital Industry," *Management Science* 58, no. 4 (2012): 708–722; and D. KC and B. R. Staats, "Accumulating a Portfolio of Experience: The Effect of Focal and Related Experience on Surgeon Performance," *Manufacturing and Service Operations Management* 14, no. 4 (2012): 618–633.

36. P. J. Hinds, "The Curse of Expertise: The Effects of Expertise and Debiasing Methods on Prediction of Novice Performance," *Journal of Experimental Psychology: Applied* 5, no. 2 (1999): 205–221.

37. T. Zhang, "Back to the Beginning: Rediscovering Inexperience Helps Experts Give Advice," Academy of Management Proceedings, Academy of Management, 2015.

Chapter 9

1. R. S. Huckman, B. R. Staats, and D. M. Upton, "Team Familiarity, Role Experience, and Performance: Evidence from Indian Software Services," *Management Science* 55, no. 1 (2009): 85–100; R. S. Huckman and B. R. Staats, "Fluid Tasks and Fluid Teams: The Impact of Diversity in Experience and Team Familiarity on Team Performance," *Manufacturing and Service Operations Management* 13, no. 3 (2011): 310–328; and B. R. Staats, "Unpacking Team Familiarity: The Effect of Geographic Location and Hierarchical Role," *Production and Operations Management* 21, no. 3 (2012): 619–635.

2. Y. Fried et al., "Job Design in Temporal Context: A Career Dynamics Perspective," *Journal of Organizational Behavior* 28 (2007): 911–927.

3. F. Herzberg, "One More Time: How Do You Motivate Employees?" *Harvard Business Review* 46, no. 1 (1968): 53–62.

4. N. I. Eisenberger, M. D. Lieberman, and K. D. Williams, "Does Rejection Hurt? An fMRI Study of Social Exclusion," *Science* 302, no. 5643 (2003): 290–292; and W. R. Hobbs et al., "Online Social Integration Is Associated with Reduced Mortality Risk," *Proceedings of the National Academy of Sciences* 113, no. 46 (2016): 12980–12984.

5. A. M. Grant and J. M. Berg, "Prosocial Motivation at Work: When, Why, and How Making a Difference Makes a Difference," in *The Oxford Handbook of Positive Organizational Scholarship*, eds. G. M. Spreitzer and K. S. Cameron (New York: Oxford University Press, 2012).

6. A. M. Grant et al., "Impact and the Art of Motivation Maintenance: The Effects of Contact with Beneficiaries on Persistence Behavior," *Organizational Behavior and Human Decision Processes* 103, no. 1 (2007): 53–67.

7. McChrystal's book, *Team of Teams*, details this learning and others from his many years of leadership experience. S. McChrystal et al., *Team of Teams: New Rules of Engagement for a Complex World* (New York: Penguin, 2015).

8. L. H. Pelled, K. M. Eisenhardt, and K. R. Xin, "Exploring the Black Box: An Analysis of Work Group Diversity, Conflict, and Performance," *Administrative Science Quarterly* 44, no. 1 (1999): 1–28; D. A. Harrison and K. J. Klein, "What's the Difference? Diversity Constructs as Separation, Variety, or Disparity in Organizations," *Academy of Management Review* 32, no. 4 (2009): 1199–1228; S. Narayanan et al., "A Matter of Balance: Specialization, Task Variety, and Individual Learning in a Software Maintenance Environment," *Management Science* 55, no. 11 (2009): 1861–1876; and M. E. Sosa, "Where Do Creative Interactions Come From? The Role of Tie Content and Social Networks," *Organization Science* 22, no. 1 (2011): 1–21.

9. Narayanan, "A Matter of Balance."

10. Sosa, "Where Do Creative Interactions Come From?"

11. A. Conti and C. Liu, "Bringing the Lab Back In: Personnel Composition and Scientific Output at the MIT Department of Biology," *Research Policy* 44 (2015): 1633–1644; C. Liu and J. Chown, "Geography and Power in an Organizational Forum: Evidence from the U.S. Senate Chamber," *Strategic Management Journal* 36, no. 2 (2015): 177–196; and C. Liu and T. Stuart, "Boundaries Awry? Knowledge Production and Social Networks in a Corporate R&D Lab," working paper, University of Toronto, 2016.

12. M. F. Wiersema and K. A. Bantel, "Top Management Team Turnover as an Adaptation Mechanism: The Role of the Environment," *Strategic Management Journal* 14, no. 7 (1993): 485–504; and D. A. Harrison and K. J. Klein "What's the Difference? Diversity Constructs as Separation, Variety, or Disparity in Organizations," *Academy of Management Review* 32, no. 4 (2007): 1199–1228.

13. C. Heath and N. Staudenmayer, "Coordination Neglect: How Lay Theories of Organizing Complicate Coordination in Organizations," *Research in Organizational Behavior* 22 (2000): 153–191.

14. B. R. Staats, K. L. Milkman, and C. Fox, "The Team Scaling Fallacy: Underestimating the Declining Efficiency of Larger Teams," *Organizational Behavior and Human Decision Processes* 118, no. 2 (2012): 132–142.

15. F. Brooks, *The Mythical Man-Month: Essays on Software Engineering* (New York: Addison-Wesley, 1975).

16. Ibid.

17. G. Stasser and W. Titus, "Pooling of Unshared Information in Group Decision Making: Biased Information Sampling During Discussion," *Journal of Personality and Social Psychology* 48, no. 6 (1985): 1467–1478; G. Stasser and W. Titus, "Effects of Information Load and Percentage of Shared Information on the Dissemination of Unshared Information During Group Discussion," *Journal of Personality and Social Psychology* 53, no. 1 (1987): 81–93; G. Stasser and L. A. Taylor, "Speaking Turns in Face-to-Face Discussions," *Journal of Personality and Social Psychology* 60, no. 5 (1991): 675–684; and G. Stasser, S. I. Vaughan, and D. D. Stewart, "Pooling Unshared Information: The Benefits of Knowing How Access to Information Is Distributed Among Group Members," *Organizational Behavior and Human Decision Processes* 82, no. 1 (2000): 102–116.

18. Pelled, "Exploring the Black Box"; P. J. Hinds et al., "Choosing Work Group Members: Balancing Similarity, Competence, and Familiarity," *Organizational Behavior and Human Decision Processes* 81, no. 2 (2000): 226–251; P. J. Hinds. and D. E. Bailey, "Out of Sight, Out of Sync: Understanding Conflict in Distributed Teams," *Organization Science* 14, no. 6 (2003): 615–632; Harrison, "What's the Difference"; and Huckman, "Fluid Tasks and Fluid Teams."

19. J. I. Krueger, "Return of the Ego—Self-Referent Information as a Filter for Social Prediction: Comment on Karniol (2003)," *Psychological Review* 110, no. 3 (2003): 585–590.

20. L. Ross, "The Intuitive Psychologist and His Shortcomings," in *Advances in Experimental Social Psychology*, ed. L. Berkowitz (San Diego, CA: Academic Press, 1977), 173–220. Amy Edmondson introduced me to the idea of naïve realism in our discussions about how to teach team collaboration. She has written more on this in her wonderful book on the topic. A. C. Edmondson, *Teaming: How Organizations Learn, Innovate, and Compete in the Knowledge Economy* (New York: John Wiley & Sons, 2012).

21. N. Epley and J. Schroeder, "Mistakenly Seeking Solitude," *Journal of Experimental Psychology: General* 143, no. 5 (2014): 1980.

22. K. Huang et al., "It Doesn't Hurt to Ask: Question-Asking Increases Liking," *Journal of Personality and Social Psychology* 113, no. 3 (2017).

23. Huckman, "Team Familiarity, Role Experience, and Performance"; Huckman, "Fluid Tasks and Fluid Teams"; H. K. Gardner, F. Gino, and B. R. Staats, "Dynamically Integrating Knowledge in Teams: Transforming Resources into

Performance," *Academy of Management Journal* 55, no. 4 (2012): 998–1022; and Staats, "Unpacking Team Familiarity."

24. It is worth noting that Booth still works to build relationships with everyone he interacts with. For example, he says that when he has a Christmas party, he invites everyone in the practice, not just the most senior people or just the doctors, as often happens in other circumstances.

25. R. Huckman and B. R. Staats, "The Hidden Benefits of Keeping Teams Intact," *Harvard Business Review* 91, no. 12 (2013): 27–29.

26. K. J. Arrow, "Classificatory Notes on the Production and Transmission of Technological Knowledge," *American Economic Review* 59, no. 2 (1969): 29–35; and K. Monteverde, "Technical Dialog as an Incentive for Vertical Integration in the Semiconductor Industry," *Management Science* 41, no. 10 (1995): 1624–1638.

27. D. M. Wegner, "Transactive Memory: A Contemporary Analysis of the Group Mind," in *Theories of Group Behavior*, eds. G. Mullen and G. Goethals (New York: Springer-Verlag, 1987), 185–208.

28. J. R. Austin, "Transactive Memory in Organizational Groups: The Effects of Content, Consensus, Specialization, and Accuracy on Group Performance," *Journal of Applied Psychology* 88, no. 5 (2003): 866–878; D. P. Brandon and A. B. Hollingshead, "Transactive Memory Systems in Organizations: Matching Tasks, Expertise, and People," *Organization Science* 15, no. 6 (2004): 633–644; K. Lewis, D. Lange, and L. Gillis, "Transactive Memory Systems, Learning, and Learning Transfer," *Organization Science* 16, no. 6 (2005): 581–598; Y. Q. Ren, K. M. Carley, and L. Argote, "The Contingent Effects of Transactive Memory: When Is It More Beneficial to Know What Others Know?" *Management Science* 52, no. 5 (2006): 671–682; and F. Gino et al., "First, Get Your Feet Wet: The Effects of Learning from Direct and Indirect Experience on Team Creativity," *Organizational Behavior and Human Decision Processes* 111, no. 2 (2010): 102–115.

29. D. H. Gruenfeld et al., "Group Composition and Decision Making: How Member Familiarity and Information Distribution Affect Process and Performance," *Organizational Behavior and Human Decision Processes* 67, no. 1 (1996): 1–15; A. C. Edmondson, R. M. Boh mer, and G. P. Pisano, "Disrupted Routines: Team Learning and New Technology Implementation in Hospitals," *Administrative Science Quarterly* 46, no. 4 (2001): 685–716; B. McEvily, V. Perrone, and A. Zaheer, "Trust as an Organizing Principle," *Organization Science* 14, no. 1 (2003): 91–103; and A. A. Kane, L. Argote, and J. M. Levine, "Knowledge Transfer Between Groups via Personnel Rotation: Effects of Social Identity and Knowledge Quality," *Organizational Behavior and Human Decision Processes* 96, no. 1 (2005): 56–71.

30. R. Katz, "The Effects of Group Longevity on Project Communication and Performance," *Administrative Science Quarterly* 27, no. 1 (1982): 81–104.

31. R. Reagans, L. Argote, and D. Brooks, "Individual Experience and Experience Working Together," *Management Science* 51, no. 6 (2005):

869–881; and Huckman, "Team Familiarity, Role Experience, and Performance."

32. D. A. Garvin and M. A. Roberto, "What You Don't Know about Making Decisions," *Harvard Business Review* 79, no. 8 (2001): 108–119.

33. L. A. Seneca, *Ad Lucilium Epistulae Morales: Books LXVI–XCII*, vol. 75 (Boston: Harvard University Press, 1920).

34. J. Clark, V. Kuppuswamy, and B. R. Staats, "Goal-Relatedness and Learning: Evidence from Hospitals," *Organization Science* (forthcoming 2017).

Index

Numbers in italics refer to pages with images.

Acknowledgments

This book is the product of many years of work—arguably a lifetime. In addition, it has been shaped by more people than I can count. I name many, here, but to any left out the fault is mine and the fact that I am, at times, an absent-minded professor. There are two people most responsible for influencing my work in this book; appropriately, I wish to start with one and finish with the other.

When I finished my MBA at Harvard Business School, I did not plan on returning to pursue my doctorate. However, life intervened, and I was left to consider what I wanted my post-MBA career to include. I had heard of a certain operations professor from the United Kingdom when I had been a student, and then my brother ended up working closely with him. And so I reached out to David Upton to discuss the idea of returning to HBS to pursue a doctorate. We hit it off immediately, and I'm sure he played an important role in my eventual admission to the program. After I was admitted, I had no doubts about the role he played in my education and path to understanding about the learning process. Dave was the mentor I aspire to be. He was thoughtful and encouraging. One of the smartest people I've ever met, he mastered every topic he sought to understand. He cared about me not only as a student, but also as a person. When we were deep in the program, he brought my young family to join his on their family vacation in Crete. He was an inspiration to me, first in my role as student and then as a professor, showing how someone who truly cared about learning could act. Dave tragically passed, far too young, in 2017. In writing this book, I had actually imagined what it would be like to present him the finished product so he could see his fingerprints all over it. Instead, I will share it with Dave's wife, his children, and his parents, and hope it might make them smile to see his obvious influence throughout it.

Professionally, I have been fortunate to work with a number of wonderful people. I have sought to work with those more talented than myself and succeeded at that task, time and time again. My other advisers at HBS, Rob Huckman and Gary Pisano, have been instrumental in my career. Gary cochaired my dissertation and helped me understand the need to approach our careers with the same operations strategy that we teach firms to apply to their own processes. Rob is not only curious and thoughtful, but he is also the empiricist that I aspire to be. Watching him, I knew that if I could approach problems with half of the rigor that he does, then I could do interesting and impactful work. Anyone reading my academic papers can see Rob's very strong influence.

Kent Bowen was one of the first faculty members with whom I worked at HBS. He helped me understand (as much as I do) what the Toyota Production System really meant for learning. Amy Edmondson is a learning scholar who practices what she preaches. Her research has taught and inspired me and it was one of the great joys to get to work with her on projects. Ananth Raman helped me understand what being an operations scholar really meant. Frances Frei has always been willing to speak hard truths to me—highlighting what I can do better. Other faculty, including Clay Christensen, Frances Frei, Giovanni Gavetti, Jan Hammond, Marco Iansiti, Andy King, Roy Shapiro, Mike Toffel, Mike Tushman, and Zeynep Ton, all helped me immeasurably in my own doctoral efforts—learning to be a researcher and a teacher. Special thanks to Max Bazerman, who I didn't come to really know until after I left HBS, for his assistance in navigating the publication process.

My coauthors in my research have all left their imprints on this book. The stories told in these pages of the research highlight the influential roles that each played. In addition to challenging me intellectually, they have become dear friends. Francesca Gino has been my most frequent coauthor through the years. She brings an inquisitiveness and joy to every project in which she engages. She served as a catalyst for me—creating opportunities to turbocharge both my own work and our collaborative work. I am incredibly grateful for our time working together. Diwas KC has helped shape my operations lens to explore problems. We met casually during his visit to UNC, and as we talked, we realized that we worked well together. Nine months later, we had an accepted paper and then we were off to the races. Katy Milkman has challenged me since grad school, and is an equally enjoyable person and coauthor. Dave Hoffman walked into my office for a sanity check that turned into a great collaboration, for which I'm very grateful. David Brunner kept me sane in grad school and has challenged me ever since. Thanks also to great partnerships with many others, including Dan Cable, Jonathan Clark, Rellie Derfler-Rozin, Seyed Emadi, Heidi Gardner, Saravanan Kesavan, Celia Moore, and Tom Tan.

I am fortunate to be at a fantastic university that values both rigor and relevance. From the leadership of our deans—Jim Dean and then Doug Shackelford—to the leadership of the faculty—Jay Swaminathan, Jennifer Conrad, and Dave Hoffman—to the leadership of the operations area—Ann Marucheck, the best boss I have ever had, and Vinayak Deshpande—I have been given the freedom, encouragement, and resources to pursue my strengths to try to make a difference for our students and practicing managers. My operations' colleagues at Kenan-Flagler have similarly played a fundamental role in keeping work fun and intellectually engaging. Special thanks go to Adam Mersereau. Even if we have not yet found a way to collaborate on a project, his willingness to listen to my ideas and complaints has been a gift. Saravanan Kesavan has been a mentor since we were at HBS together and has been a wonderful colleague and collaborator, as well as a friend. Thanks go to other faculty, including Seyed Emadi, Wendell Gilland, Lauren Lu, Ali Parlakturk, Nur Sunar, Sandeep Rath, and the late Harvey Wagner.

In the lead-up to writing this book, I had the good fortune to spend a year at the Wharton School as visiting faculty. That created the opportunity not only to work with Katy Milkman in person again, but to get to know one of my academic idols—Christian Terwiesch. Christian's work was an inspiration to me, so it was incredibly exciting to call him a colleague and eventually a collaborator. Not only did he help me when we were colleagues, but many years before, he had served as an editor on a paper of mine and truly taught me what it meant to be an empirical operations scholar. At some point, I hope, we will get to work on a serious project together. Long conversations with Gerard Cachon similarly challenged my worldview on how operations really work. I am grateful for the time spent around Marshall Fisher, from whom I cannot help but learn when I'm near. Simone Marinesi was a treat to teach (and frequently share coffee) with, and I enjoyed my interactions with other faculty, including Morris Cohen, Noah Gans, Cade Massey, Maurice Schweitzer, and Senthil Veeraraghavan.

My research has been fundamentally shaped by the students I have worked with. Doctoral students Ethan Bernstein, Hengchen Dai, Maria Ibanez, R.J. Niewoehner, Pradeep Pendem, and Melissa Valentine have taught me as much as I taught them. I've been lucky enough to teach many MBA and executive development participants who have not only allowed me to test my ideas, but also helped to create new ones.

As I was conceiving the idea of this book, I wanted to test it with the target audience. That meant turning to my friends, who were kind enough to generously spend time with me discussing the topic. Schuyler Jones and John Stillson not only spent many hours with me on the baseball field, but were also willing to share their own experiences (and then, in Schuyler's case, to review my storytelling in the cardiology example that I use to make sure I did not sound foolish). Greg Bromberger, Chris Crane, Kyle Chenet, Andy Greene, and Steve McMahon were similarly generous with their time.

Before entering academia, I had often read about how important editors were to the writing process. I believed that to be true—if everyone was saying it, then it must be so. However, I had no way to really know if that was the case. I have now had the opportunity to work with two truly great editors. The first is Steve Prokesch. Steve takes anything I give him and pushes me to make it better. His willingness to let me get away with throwaway lines and wasted space is zero. It is the type of behavior that may be annoying when you are rushing to hit a deadline, but it is immeasurably valuable when you are trying to have long-term impact. Tim Sullivan, my editor on this book, guided this novice author through the process. He has walked the fine line of letting my voice come through while at the same time pushing me to improve my work. Any mistakes left are my own. I cannot say enough positive things about working with him and the entire HBR Press team. Special thanks to Martha Spaulding for doing a wonderful job copyediting the book. Thanks to Jennifer Waring and Jon Shipley, as well.

Throughout my life, I have been surrounded by more great educators than I can list. They nurtured a young boy's passion for English and math and helped me to find a place I could be comfortable. Growing up in the Eanes Independent School District I was spoiled to get to learn from teachers such as Mrs. Calvert, Mrs. Sassano, Mrs. Andrus, Mr. Batt, Mrs. Browne, Mrs. Blair, Mr. Harper, Mrs. Flatau, and Coach Hinojosa. At the University of Texas, special thanks goes to Kurt Heinzelman—for utterly destroying my writing, but then building it back up—and Mack Grady, who was a patient, encouraging mentor with whom I loved working in electrical engineering. Thanks also go to Dean Ben Streetman for his help both during my time at UT and afterward.

I never would have found myself on the path to this book without my family. My mother has always been my strongest supporter. She not only believed that her sons could do anything that they set their minds to, but she was always there to support us in the effort. This encouragement was empowering. Her going back to school when I was a child, and then managing everything in her life while still always having time for me, made it clear that I too could work toward whatever I dreamed. My father has been the individual that I most looked up to throughout my life. He has set an example for how to achieve excellence while treating people well. I always knew that he was busy, but that he would make whatever time I needed. My older brother, Trent, is one of the most accomplished people that I know. He was always an inspiration to me, and even as a child, he always looked to help his younger brother. Knowing that someone of his talents (and size) had my back created a comfort level that I cannot describe. Except for one traumatic game of Atari baseball, Trent tried to make my life easier, while challenging me to still be my best. Thanks go to my Uncle Glenn and Aunt Marsha as well for setting examples on how hard work and learning could create opportunities for anyone. My in-laws have been in my life now for longer than they were not. I'm grateful to Rick for sharing his perspectives on learning lessons and making his long list of contacts available to me. Becky has been an encourager for as long as I have known her. Moreover, I am not sure we would have made it through the early years of parenthood without her help. Thank you.

Finally, I need to thank the four people I spend the most time with. Our three sons are constantly an inspiration for me to learn. Each was born when I was a doctoral student, and my wife and I would joke that even if academia did not work out, at least we had something to show for grad school. Watching them as they navigate these learning-rich years, I am amazed. They are inquisitive, kind, and energetic. I cannot believe my good fortune to have them around to call me "Dad." I hope that they will learn as much from me as I have had the opportunity to learn from them.

I end this section with the other person who deserves the most credit for this book's creation—Patricia Cantwell Staats. Tricia and I met on Halloween of our freshman year at Texas. I still don't know what she saw in an awkward, socially clueless boy, but I'm grateful she saw it. Through many changes, many cities, and many years, she is a joy to be around. She is intelligent, thoughtful, and kind. She knows how to act in whatever situation she finds herself and is the type of person you feel so comfortable with that you immediately tell her your deepest secrets. She not only has believed in me and supported me in accomplishing my goals and our family's goals, but she makes me want to be a better person. I know that I won't always succeed at that, but when I fall short, she is there to help me learn from the failure and move on in a productive direction.

> No love, no friendship
> can cross the path of our destiny
> without leaving
> some mark on it forever—
> I'm so thankful
> Your path
> Has crossed mine.
>
> **—François Mauriac**

Almost twenty-five years later, I'm still thankful that our paths crossed. We may have begun with the naïveté of youth, but I could not imagine a better partner with whom to spend my life. May we never stop learning together.

About the Author

BRADLEY R. STAATS, DBA, is a professor at the University of North Carolina Kenan-Flagler Business School. He works with individuals and organizations seeking to learn and improve in order to stay relevant, innovate, and succeed on an ongoing basis. His teaching focuses on how to design organizations that are able to continuously learn as well as how to incorporate analytics so that data can drive decision making. In addition to teaching at UNC Kenan-Flagler, he works with companies around the world on their learning and analytics strategies.

Staats's research investigates the role of human behavior in learning and operational improvement. He integrates work in operations management and behavioral science to understand how and under what conditions individuals, teams, and organizations perform at their best. He conducts field research in settings such as health care and software services, consulting, call centers, and retail. He uses archival data and field experiments to provide an interdisciplinary perspective to improve both theory and practice.

Staats publishes frequently in and serves on the editorial boards of several leading academic journals. His work has also been featured in a variety of media outlets. He has won numerous teaching and research awards, including the Wickham Skinner Early-Career Research Accomplishments Award from the Production and Operations Management

Society, the Poets & Quants award as one of the "Best 40 Under 40" business school professors in the world, and the Warren Bennis Prize for best article in *Harvard Business Review* on leadership.

Staats earned both his DBA (in technology and operations management) and his MBA from Harvard Business School. He received his BS degree, with honors, in electrical engineering and his BA degree, with high honors, in Plan II and Spanish from the University of Texas at Austin, where he was named the Most Outstanding Male Graduate of his graduating class.

Prior to his academic career, Staats worked as a venture capitalist at a leading firm in the southeastern United States. He also worked in investment banking at Goldman Sachs and strategic planning at Dell.

Staats lives in Chapel Hill with his wife and three sons. He can frequently be found on local playing fields helping coach his kids' baseball teams.